CW01468586

# In and Out of Africa

Copyright © ( Sarah Jewell 2021 )

ISBN: 978-178456-786-6
Paperback

First published 2021 by Upfront Publishing
Peterborough, England.

An environmentally friendly book printed and bound in England
by www.printondemand-worldwide.com

# In and Out of Africa

## Memoirs of
Peter Jewell and
Juliet Clutton-Brock

By Sarah Jewell

Design by Jessica Ballard

With thanks to my sisters,
Topsy and Rebecca,
for their encouragement and ideas;
to my husband, Andy, for his tech support;
and to Jessica Ballard
for her beautiful book design.

Written in loving memory of my parents

# Contents

Foreword      8

1   Tenderness and tragedy:      12
Juliet's early childhood

2   Goldfish, picnics and birdwatching:      28
Peter's childhood and wartime evacuation

3   Into Africa:      50
Juliet's wartime evacuation

4   Cold porridge and sea swimming:      66
Juliet's school days and Jacobean home life

5   Farming, fishing and physiology:      74
Peter's student days

6   From Vet school to the Zoo:      84
Peter's early career and marriage to Juliet

7  Pottery, the Natural History Museum and          98
archaeozoology: Juliet's early career

8  Civil war, a mini zoo and ecology:              106
Biafra 1966

9  Field trips, hazy days and evacuation:          124
Biafra 1967

10  Old bones, skeletons and dogs:                 138
Juliet's career takes off

11  Lectures, giraffes and professorship:          144
Peter's career progresses

12  School days and holidays:                      158
family life in Highgate, Hampstead and Gwithian

13  Retirement, Cambridge and the Fens:            172
the final years

# Foreword

P eter and Juliet were two intrepid zoologists who lived extraordinary lives. They were brilliant, dedicated, brave, adventurous and irascible. Together they were a team in their shared academic interests and passion for animals, but outside of work they were very different – Peter was the great, gregarious, confident communicator and Juliet the introverted, reclusive intellectual. They both had traumatic events in their childhoods, as a result of the second world war and their family situations, but they overcame these challenges through grit and determination, and together went on to achieve great success in the fields of animal research and archaeozoology.

The overriding passion they shared was a love of animals and of Africa. Juliet grew up in Zimbabwe (then Rhodesia), they lived in Nigeria and were caught up in the Biafran war; Peter studied large mammals in Uganda and Kenya, and they both travelled extensively throughout the continent. Wherever they lived, from Highgate to Cornwall to Nigeria to Hampstead to Cambridge, animals filled their lives. In England they were surrounded by dogs, hamsters, cats, tortoises, goldfish, catfish, bantams, and donkeys; in Africa, it was chameleons, a chimpanzee, angwantibos,

Juliet and Peter with their dogs, Jess and Lucie, in Cornwall

pottos, a python and little dik-dik. Every conversation was punctuated with an admonishment or affectionate pat to one of the dogs, and these conversations usually centred around animal behaviour and welfare – ranging from the domestication of the dog, to bluetits nesting in the garden, to the mating behaviour of Soay sheep on St Kilda and antelope in Uganda.

Juliet always looked elegant, she had a smart, crisp bob and her hair was soft brown and in later life streaked with grey. She wore long flowing skirts and silk blouses, and loved autumnal colours – browns, greens, maroons and dark reds. She wore beautiful jewellery that she had inherited from her mother and grandmother – long amber beads, navy blue opals and a green glass ring with an engraving of a dog on it. She had very dark-brown eyes and wore spectacles, and as the frames were quite large they looked owlish on her small, delicate face. She loved walking and always took the dogs with her. In the foreword of her last book, *Animals as Domesticates*, she wrote: "This was written with the memory of all the animals who have been my companions over the years, beginning with my Rhodesian Ridgeback, Zimba, in 1941." And there were many more dogs to come – after Zimba there was Torf the whippet, Rags the Yorkshire terrier, Lucie a white and tan sheepdog crossbreed, Jess the black and tan mongrel, Jack – son of Jess, Bruno the chocolate labrador and finally Sylvie the English setter.

Peter also enjoyed living in a house full of pets and cared deeply about protecting animals in their natural environment. His heroes were Charles Darwin and William Morris, and he hung two huge photos of them on the walls of his study. Morris's dictum "own nothing that you do not know to be beautiful or believe to be useful" was the rule by which both he and Juliet lived. Peter had a passion for arts and crafts, and collected paintings by Cornish artists, pottery by Bernard Leach and treasures from the Arts and Crafts movement. He was a champion of workers' rights and a socialist. He was always stylish in his appearance and had a fantastic collection of waistcoats and handmade silk and woven ties in reds, pinks and greens.

Together they made a formidable couple and their adventurous and dynamic life stories are inspirational.

Juliet and Peter at their cottage in Gwithian, Cornwall

# Tenderness and tragedy: Juliet's early childhood

# I

J uliet was born on 16 September 1933 at the Stonefield Nursing Home in Greenwich, south London. She was the elder child of Sheelah Mabel Stoney Archer and Alan Francis Clutton-Brock. They lived in Greenwich in a large Georgian house, high above the Thames on the edge of Blackheath. Alan was a slim aesthete with a long, bony face and a dry wit, while Sheelah was a brilliant and beautiful scholar. They met at Cambridge where Sheelah was at Newnham College reading economics and Alan was at King's College studying classics. Sheelah's sister Kathleen recalled how Sheelah's friends made her undress in the moonlight and stand silhouetted on the bow of a punt for them all to marvel at. Alan was madly in love with her and desperate to get married.

However, they had a long struggle to tie the knot as Alan's mother strongly disapproved of Sheelah and would not allow them to meet at her house. In his letter of 17 August 1925, Alan writes to Sheelah saying:

*"I have told my mother about you and she got into a great fluster and thought I might be going to marry you. She seemed to take it*

more hardly than one might have suspected. I can't write – and will tell you all that she said when we get to Cambridge, which, thank God is not very far ahead. She has made me promise not to live with you again til I come down from Cambridge."

Alan explained to Sheelah that his mother thought they would tire of each other, but "in that respect, I am sure she will be disappointed. Perhaps I ought not to have told my mother but I was rather unhappy at having to continue deceiving her. I feel perhaps I have treated you badly over this promise but my dear I would wait years and years for you if it was essential."

On 1 May 1926 Alan wrote from his house at 28 Oakley Street, Chelsea, to Sheelah saying how much he wanted to be with her:

"It will be heaven to see you. How I long for you my dearest, dearest, Sheelah. I suppose it would be difficult to go away from your family and an excuse would be hard but you must contrive to do so soon, sometime when my mother is safely packed away for the weekend. I believe I might come to see you, if you can get your parents to be so long suffering, for the weekend after. Til Friday my darling one then, not that I shall not write to you in the meanwhile. But I am all afire to see you. I want you closer, and closer so that we touch in all ways, that we are one flesh and one mind. I love you, I love you, your Alan."

And in another letter he says:

"Whatever happens I must see you soon, it is a vital necessity of my life – I feel as if I had been cut off from food or air without you. Well that's a hyperbole but I mean really that without you I feel all the while a great gap in myself, as if, say, I had lost a leg. Oh my dear my dear come back to me soon. I can't live without you your most loving Alan."

Sheelah divided her time between Cambridge and her family home in Cheltenham and found the situation difficult. One of her school friends from Roedean who described herself as "your unintelligent little friend Doris", wrote to Sheelah saying:

"I hear that your nerves have been in a shocking state and a great anxiety to all your friends and relatives. You have my sympathy do you overwork terribly? The last I heard of you was that you spent many hours daily lying on a sofa, gazing at futurist drawings, sipping tea and talking to economists, smoking meanwhile a most expensive brand of cigarettes. The description terrified me – oh yes, and your Kathleen [Sheelah's older sister] met a young man in Paris who said you looked like a picture by Botticelli."

In another passionate letter to Sheelah, Alan describes his remorse at feeling uncomfortable and guilty when they went to a hotel together and the proprietor made him feel so nervous he fled, when all he really wanted was to be with her:

"Oh but I am your lover, I could be happy for ever to kiss your beautiful breast and to clasp your warm firm body in my arms and to be so near to you that every one of my limbs is against one of yours. And to lie beside you and talk to you of our love, what more could I want? You are my darling companion it is true but *you are also a being whom I passionately long to hold, to crush against me and to feel you and I are a universe in ourselves."*

Alan came from a wealthy and long-established literary background. He was born in Weybridge, Surrey, on 8 October 1904, and was the son of Arthur Clutton-Brock and his wife, Evelyn Alice Clutton-Brock (nee Vernon-Harcourt). Evelyn was an artist and the daughter of civil engineer Leveson Francis Vernon-Harcourt while Arthur was an author and critic. They lived at Farncombe Lodge, Godalming, Surrey, and later at the Red House, Godalming, a beautiful early Edwin Lutyens house where Evelyn painted the doorframes and bannisters with colourful little flower motifs. Alan followed in his father's footsteps and went to Eton as a King's scholar in April 1919, where

Alan and Sheelah at Cambridge, photo by Ramsey and Muspratt, 1935

he did not have a happy time but won several prizes for art and English. He started his degree in classics at Cambridge but changed to English.

Sheelah was the eldest daughter of Lt Col George Johnston Stoney Archer, an army surgeon who served during the Boer War, and Ethel Mary Archer (nee Beauchamp). They both came from old Irish families and Ethel was the daughter of Robert Beauchamp, an Irish judge, and his wife Gertrude. She had one sister, Mabel, who Juliet knew as Aunty Mabs. After Sheelah was born on 19 July 1903 (in Jamaica), George and Ethel had three other children, Kathleen Gertrude, Robert Stoney and Doreen Sylvia.

Despite his mother's opposition, Alan and Sheelah's romance continued and in 1928 they were married. Five years later, after a seriously dangerous miscarriage and illness, Sheelah gave birth to Juliet and the family moved to The Manor House, Crooms Hill, Greenwich. Sheelah

Alan as a young man, painted by his mother

was a very loving mother and spent a lot of time reading and researching how to care for her newborn baby.

In order of age, from back – Sheelah, Kathleen, Robert, Doreen, 1913

Alan wanted to be an artist and spent his time painting – he studied at Westminster School of Art and was influenced by Constable and the French impressionists, but his landscapes and still lifes did not sell well so he was constantly in debt. He joined The Times in 1930 as a writer and contributed to The Times Literary Supplement. He also published books including *Italian Painting* (1930), *An Introduction to French Painting* (1932), *Blake, a short life of William Blake* (1933) and a novel, *Murder at Liberty Hall* (1941).

Sheelah, painted by her mother Ethel

Still lifes by Alan,
top left and bottom

On 22 August 1935 Juliet's brother Francis was born. Sheelah was concerned about her baby son's weight so she wrote to Nursery World magazine to ask for advice, and on 18 October 1935 received this reply:

*"Dear Mrs Clutton-Brock, I am interested to hear of your baby son. According to his theoretical caloric requirement he is due for a total of 27ozs in the day. Breast-fed babies as a matter of fact usually gain satisfactorily when having less than their theoretical requirement. Your baby would probably progress well on only 26ozs. Baby's restlessness and the condition of his stools show that he is having more food than he can comfortably digest. Temporarily give about five minutes before each feed, one teaspoon of dill water in one ounce of warm boiled water, helping him to get up wind before putting him to the breast. Allow at present slightly shorter feeds."*

But the cosy family life was about to be shattered. One day a few months later, Sheelah made a fateful decision to go out for a drive with a friend –

and the lives of Juliet and Francis were changed for ever. On Tuesday, 7 January 1936, Sheelah had been at home all day, at the Manor House in Greenwich, looking after Juliet and Francis, who were both ill. Later, she decided to join her friend, Dr Norman Dyer Ball, 39, for a drive in his Morris-Cowley saloon. He had been the family doctor and she first met him when he had his surgery at Crooms Hill in Greenwich. Dr Ball ran

Juliet aged 18 months, by Ramsey and Muspratt

Sheelah and her mother's dog Beau

the surgery with his wife Doris Ball who was also a doctor – and became a crime writer under the name of Josephine Bell. Sheelah and Norman became close friends, possibly lovers.

Dr Ball had recently given up his GP practice due to ill health and was about to go on a long voyage as a ship's doctor, and had been staying with his mother in Bromley. Sheelah and Dr Ball were driving fast in wet and windy conditions along Rochesterway, Bexley, near the Gravel Hill and Bourne Road crossing, when a tragic accident occurred – the car hit the grassy verge, spun out of control across the road and hit a stationary lorry. Sheelah was half thrown out of the car and killed instantly. Ball had a fractured skull and died later in hospital. It was later suggested that perhaps he didn't understand how to handle a car with hydraulic brakes. He also had sight in only one eye as he'd lost the other in an accident during the first world war.

On Saturday, 8 February 1936, Sheelah's sister Kathleen wrote from South Africa, where she was living, to her mother about the devastating news that Sheelah had been killed in the crash.

*"My very dearest Mummy, it is unnecessary for me to tell you how terribly I feel Sheelah's death as it is for you to tell me, and I'm not going to write about her now, we will be able to talk about her later; we must all feel the same about her and what she meant to us personally, and to her children, and to Alan; and what her own life meant to her. The thing for me to do now is to think about you, and when I am home about her children. Your calmly written letter (in spite of what your feelings must have been) came as some comfort after I had heard the news by cable the same day. I was in Durban and rang up nanny to say I could not get back that night, she told me of the wire and I got her to read it out. I was profoundly shocked I could scarcely speak but got her to send someone from the hotel to fetch me. How lucky for you that Gladys was with you at the time you heard the news, but you must have had a most ghastly blow, I hope Alan phoned you or his mother and that you didn't get a wire, you were very courageous to motor up at once. Lots and lots and lots of love my dearest mummy from Kathleen"*

The car in which Mrs. Clifton-Brock was killed instantly, and her companion, Dr. Norman Dyer Ball, died in hospital, after their car had come into collision with a lorry at Rochester Road, Bexley Heath.

Sheelah's accident and death were reported in the newspapers at the time in great detail. In one cutting "Double fatality at Gravel Hill – Doctor and Friend killed", the reporter describes how Dr Ball was driving a 12hp Morris-Cowley saloon car which he had hired. According to an eye-witness, at a point about 150 yards west of the crossroads, "the car which was proceeding in the direction of Dartford, mounted the kerb, careered along the grass verge, swung back into the road, skidded round two or three times, and struck a stationary lorry broadside. The lorry was a Fordson gas tanker belonging to the South Suburban Gas Company, Lower Sydenham. The driver, Mr George Daughtry, of Shrimpton Square, London, noticed that the car was out of control and pulled up. His mate jumped off the lorry. The impact took place. It is stated that the car nearly went over the top of the lorry and then overturned. The two off-side doors were torn right off, the body of the car was knocked off the chassis, the roof was smashed, and part subsequently was used as a stretcher. The body of Mrs Clutton-Brock was removed to the mortuary at Bexley Heath and Dr Ball was taken to the County Hospital, Dartford, where it was found that he had sustained a fracture of the base of the skull."

An extract from the Kentish Times of 17 January 1933 reports on the inquest into Sheelah's death,

Sheelah at Cambridge

which said that she was "killed instantly when the car in which she was a passenger crashed into a stationary lorry" and that a "verdict of Death from Misadventure was returned in the case of the doctor and accidental death in regard of Mrs Clutton-Brock".

George Orwell, who had been at Eton with Alan, wrote in a letter in 1936 to a friend:

> "I suppose you heard about Alan Clutton-Brock's wife? A bad job, & he has two small kids, too – just recently she was killed in a motor smash." (source: the Passing Tramp, Wandering through the mystery genre, book by book)

Sheelah had made two close friends at Cambridge, Portia Holman and Marjorie Sisson. Portia had a house in Bloomsbury, 52 Gordon Square, and after Sheelah died, Alan often visited her there. Barbara Foy Mitchell was a student, aged 22, studying chemistry at UCL, and was a lodger in Portia's house where she met Alan. They fell in love and Alan proposed to her at the Ivy. They married in the summer of 1936 and had their daughter, Eleanor, in 1946. Alan and Barbara enjoyed living in Chelsea and Primrose Hill, and mixed widely in literary and artistic circles – their friends included the painter Sir William Coldstream, George Orwell, EM Forster and Stevie Smith.

During these years in London, Juliet was often looked after by Evelyn Clutton-Brock, her London granny, who had a house in Oakley Street, Chelsea. Juliet remembered being taken there after she fell off a tricycle when riding round the Round Pond in Kensington Gardens and broke her left arm above the elbow. "I was put on a bed in a small bedroom, was given chloroform and my arm was set in plaster by a doctor who had been summoned to the house."

Evelyn took Juliet on trips around London and she much enjoyed going to the Tower of London to see the ravens. "At this time also my father took me to the London Zoo and I remember sitting on a bench

Juliet and Francis painted by their grandmother Evelyn Clutton-Brock

with him where he explained that we had all evolved from monkeys. My grandmother said later that I had been disappointed that I had not seen any ravens at the Zoo, although actually there were ravens there in a specially built ironwork 'house'."

In 1938 the family went to live for a year in Chastleton House, a beautiful huge Jacobean manor near Moreton-in-Marsh, Gloucestershire, where they stayed with Alan's cousin, Irene Whitmore-Jones, who owned the house. It was always known that Alan would inherit Chastleton from her, as he was her closest, last remaining male relative and the house had been passed down through the family since it was built in 1603 by Walter Jones, a Welsh wool merchant and his wife Elinor Pope.

Walter bought the estate of Chastleton from Robert Catesby – the leader of the Gunpowder plot of 5 November 1605 against James I. Catesby had previously been involved in the 1601 failed rebellion of the Earl of Essex to remove Elizabeth I from power and was fined the huge sum of 4,000 marks. To raise this amount, he sold his house and land to Walter Jones.

In 1603 Walter Jones made the last payment for the property and the connection with the Catesby's came to an end. The old house was demolished and Chastleton was built.

As the house passed through the generations, the family became increasingly impoverished until by the time Irene inherited it there was no money left for the upkeep and repairs, or the enormous running costs. During the year that the family spent at Chastleton, the house was visited by Queen Mary, grandmother of Elizabeth II. When she arrived, Juliet had to present her with a bouquet, an honour she remembered with chagrin: "Apparently I had been trained to curtsey and after giving the Queen the bouquet I kept curtseying, and the people around me laughed – I have never been able to curtsey ever since and I believe this episode helped to make me shy for life."

Uncle Robert and his plane

During this year Juliet also had her fifth birthday, which she re-membered well because her Uncle Robert (Sheelah's brother), who was a pilot, flew over Chastleton in a small light aircraft and dropped a present for her. "We watched for it on the tower of the house and it fell in the box garden," she later said.

Juliet also recalled how she, Francis and the nanny used the pantry as their sitting room: "The nanny was frightened of the dark and used

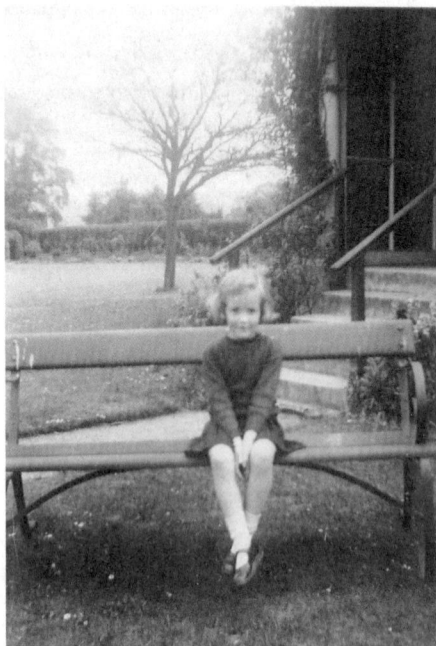
Juliet at Connelmore

to send me upstairs to the top floor, where we slept, for things that she needed for her sewing. I enjoyed this and used to look out for the owl that flew around at the top of the house and sat on one of the stair posts."

In 1939 Francis and Juliet and the nanny went to live with Sheelah's parents at their house Connelmore, in Cheltenham, which Juliet described as "a comfortable Victorian house with a large garden and an English setter called Beau. My grandfather had beehives and there were wonderful shrubberies in the garden in which to play." Juliet loved staying in Cheltenham with her Granny Ethel and remembered walking to nursery school there: "I enjoyed the walks because we often met a golden cocker spaniel called Leo with his owner and I was allowed to hold him on his lead."

However, momentous historical events were taking place and on 3 September war was declared. Juliet remembered being taken into her grandfather's study "to listen to the announcement on the news". Later she was given a gas mask with a "beautiful blue velvet box that matched the blue coat, hat and gaiters that I wore for going out in".

Chastleton House, Gloucestershire

# Goldfish, picnics and birdwatching: Peter's childhood and wartime evacuation

# 2

P eter Arundel Jewell was nine years older than Juliet and came from a very different family background. He was born on 16 June 1925 in Burntwood Lane, Tooting, and had an idea that he was destined for greater things than a humdrum life in south London. As he wrote in his memoirs: "I would like to think that at my nativity the front of heaven was full of fiery shapes and burning cressets and the goats ran from the mountain [Henry IV Part I] – but I don't suppose they did." He was the second child of Percy Arundel Jewell and Ivy Ennis – his elder sister Pamela (Pam) was born on 5 December 1922.

His father Percy (1886-1958), worked in the family carpentry business in Wandsworth and came from a large family. Peter's grandfather, Richard Arundel Jewell (1836-1914), married Susan Segrott (1844-1924) and they had 10 children – Elizabeth Ann (Annie), Susanna Grace (Bobo), Ada, Emily Arundel, Nellie, Daisy, Ethel Arundel, Richard Thomas Arundel, Percy Arundel and Dorothy Minette (Dolly). They lived in Fairfield Street, around the corner from the Grapes pub and Richard had his name over the door of the house.

Peter was a bright, sensitive child and as he described himself: "I was

Percy and Ivy on their wedding day

Richard Arundel Jewell, seated in the centre, with his family.
Percy is standing on the right behind him wearing a tie

Fairfield Street

regarded at school as a sort of 'goody' – I wasn't one of the rough, knock-about boys, who were always fighting in the playground. I was studious and good at most subjects." Soon after Peter was born the family moved to 40 Lebanon Gardens in Wandsworth, which had a big garden with a lawn and an apple tree. Percy bought the house from his sister Ethel and her husband Tom Hardwick, and the house next door was owned by Tom's sister, Auntie Nellie, who "had an even bigger garden with a big walnut tree, a pear tree and a mulberry tree". There was a gate between the gardens and Pam and Peter used to love playing next door "especially when Auntie Nellie was away".

Peter's love of animals started early and at the bottom of the garden there was a garden shed in which he kept jam jars, fishing nets and his white mice: "They were too smelly to be in the house, but I fear they died of cold one winter." He had strong memories of being in the house: "I can remember the curtains very well, lovely sweet peas billowing gently from the open window. But, of course, the curtains were thin and I would have to go to bed and lie there, and I could hear my father mowing or voices in the garden and I can remember hearing the cooing of woodpigeons as I fell off to sleep."

Peter had a negative view of his father, always describing him as a curmudgeonly old miser who never supported his academic ambitions. But Percy did foster Peter's love of animals from a very early age, starting with the construction of a goldfish pond. As Peter described it: "In the garden there was quite a deep pond which my father had dug by his workmen, with goldfish in it and a few water plants, and we used to go and get frogs and put frogs' spawn in and toads. They all thrived there."

When Peter was a bit older he went fishing with his father in the river Thames at Walton and caught a perch about 10 inches long, which he put in the pond. "I don't know why my father agreed to that because he must have thought that it would eat the goldfish, perhaps he wanted to get rid of the goldfish," Peter said.

"Anyway it didn't eat the goldfish for a long time, and we found that what it really liked was shrimps, I mean pink cooked shrimps. If you dropped a cooked shrimp in you would watch it falling in the water, the water went dark around the shrimp and suddenly it would disappear, and it was eaten up by the perch. This went on for months and then suddenly we started losing some of the small goldfish, and we realised that the perch was killing and eating them so we took him back to the river and let him go."

Percy Jewell

They also kept budgerigars: "We simply wired off the end section of the veranda that was next to the French windows leading out of the living room – my father had his carpenters come and do it

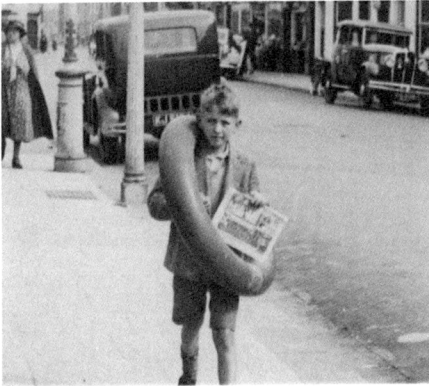
1934, Peter in Bognor Regis

nicely and properly, and put up some nest boxes, and the budgies bred like anything. The budgerigars went on breeding into the winter and we had to put an electric fire in the aviary because it felt a bit too cold for the nestlings, and so it was a bit chaotic with all that. I don't know why they went on breeding, perhaps because they were right next to the living room and got the light in the evening. Normally birds stop breeding in the winter."

The family usually spent their holidays in Worthing or Brighton, the nearest points on the south coast so this was the shortest distance Percy could possibly have to drive and therefore, according to Peter, "the least expensive excursion to make". They drove in their Standard car with an open top that folded back, a running board and mica windows that could be removed. As Peter recalled: "It was a glorious car to drive about in. Dad never drove more than 35 miles per hour and so it took us ages to get from London to Worthing – about 60 miles – especially considering that we always broke the journey for a picnic." Percy didn't believe in sitting on the ground or anything as casual as that, so the family always took their "special folding picnic table with stools that folded up inside it, a table cloth, knives and forks, plates, cups and saucers".

The family would find a place on the Downs and unpack their picnic – Ivy had to make all the food, cutting the bread and buttering it, making cucumber and tomato sandwiches and handing round the hard-boiled eggs. Then she packed it all up again in the picnic basket and on they'd go – they would stay in a place called "accommodation" with bedrooms and a dining room but they would do the shopping for food and bring it back to the landlady who cooked it for them.

According to Peter, Percy like the arrangement because this was "the cheapest kind of holiday you could have", all you paid for was the room and the landlady cooking for you, but Peter remembered the family having "arguments with the disgruntled landladies, and it was hardly a holiday for my mother".

Peter and Pam used to build sandcastles and go in for competitions on the beach. Peter won several – for building a sandcastle or making a drawing in the sand with stones. He remembered queuing up once to get a prize and to his horror it was "a pair of hairbrushes in a leather case, which I kept for donkey's years, about 20 years or more, but of course I wasn't the sort of person who used hairbrushes".

Peter and Pam at the seaside

When Peter and Pam were a bit older they went to Teignmouth by themselves – where they had three aunts and an uncle. They stayed with Auntie Susie and Auntie Dolly in their bungalow, Briar Rose, at 39 Pennyacre Road. To get there they enjoyed a magical journey by steam train from Paddington,

Five of Peter's aunts (Dorothy second from right)

through the West Country, and then, "most exciting of all", along the track right next to the sea through Dawlish and beside the red sandstone cliffs to Teignmouth.

Peter recalled: "We saw lots of sea birds and once a kingfisher. Those holidays threw Pam and I very close together. We had to stand up to our kind but strict Auntie Susie, help Auntie Dolly in the garden and go for long Sunday walks with Uncle Albert on Haldon Moor."

Peter and Pam's mother Ivy had always suffered from depression but it was largely undiagnosed. In 1937, when Peter was 12, she got into a melancholic state and her mental health started to deteriorate. The first serious episode occurred when they were on holiday in Dorset and Ivy felt so depressed and unwell that they had to cut the holiday short. Peter described how when she got home she went to see her doctor, "a man named Dr Roe, an oldish, middle-aged doctor in whom she had confidence and he gave her Sanatogen tonic wine and that was all the treatment she got".

The following year Ivy had a complete nervous breakdown and was admitted to Dartford Mental Hospital, in east London. Her mother, Amy Ennis, went to live with the family to look after the children and Ivy came back occasionally for weekends – they were always hopeful that she would come home permanently, but she never did.

Peter and Pam would go to Dartford to visit her at weekends with their father, and Peter recalled that "in a curious way those were memorable times for me because when we went to Dartford we always drove off for a picnic in the countryside somewhere, often into woods and places with lots of natural history that I would never have encountered otherwise". He used to look out for birds, ants' nests and wildflowers,

Peter at London Zoo

and enjoyed driving through the country lanes in Kent seeing the apple orchards.

By 1938 Peter was at Wandsworth secondary school and had started learning biology, which he loved, and his dissections of mice and rats impressed the biology master. He kept a diary during this time and the entries show how his passion for biology grew. The diary is printed by the Associated Builders Merchants Ltd and must have been a present from Percy. The notes he made also detail his love of visiting London Zoo to see the animals.

On Wednesday, 4 January 1939, Peter wrote that it was a rainy day but "nevertheless went to the zoo with Pam – left home 10.45 went

Pam and Peter

into aquarium and enjoyed ourselves". So many of his thoughts revolve around his visits to the zoo. And it's not just the zoo he visits – he also goes to museums. On Saturday, 27 May, he wrote: "Had a mishap with my bike this morn bent pedal went to Dartford and visited museum. Found out what my fossil was – a sea urchin." Much of early summer Peter spent walking and birdwatching on Wandsworth Common, which was a short distance from his house in Lebanon Gardens.

On Sun, 28 May, he wrote – "went for walk over common – thrush was on its nest"

Wed, 7 June – "we watched for bluetits this evening Dad and Pam saw two going in and out (of the nest)"

Fri, 9 June – "in biology I made a slide of leaf tissue for the form to see and for homework we had to describe the flowers of three trees"

Sat, 10 June – "the tits are very busy in nest box I have seen one young one on perch"

Sun, 11 June – "went on the Common this morning to get flowers of trees for biology homework"

Friday, 16 June, was Peter's 14th birthday and he described his presents: "Had telescope, torch, fish tank and money for my birthday today. Jack, John, Raymond came to grand tea went on common and played cricket this eve."

The next day he went to the bank with his birthday money – "took £1 down to bank this morn have £19 in bank now. Went with Pa to Kingston market this aft bought some plants with dad." A couple of months later, on Monday, 7 August, he spent time working on a stand for his new telescope, writing "finished my telescope stand today. Went to Headley common this evening in car with mum and I caught several newts, went flower collecting, Pam saw snake, lovely time."

By late August war was looming and it was decided that Peter and Pam should be evacuated because of the fear of bombing. Percy packed up their gas masks, name tags and sandwiches, and a bag with a few clothes. They had no idea where they were going to be sent.

A 1939 drawing by Peter

On Thursday, 31 August, Peter wrote – "we were told we would have to evacuate tomorrow so I did some shopping at Clapham Junction, this evening got a few things together"

*Fri, 1 Sept – "up at 6.20am and at school by 7.30am went to Wimbledon and then to Woking and now we are at Horsell with a nice lady. I shared with John and another boy is with us"*

Pam's school was also evacuated to Woking and she found herself living nearby. The next day Peter was sent to help build up defences:

*Sat, 2 Sept – "went to report to the local school at 9.30am this morn, ordered for meeting this aft at 2pm and went to sand pit to fill sand bags, Dad came down to see me. Dad also brought my telescope and a ball. Must write to mum this eve"*

*The next day, Sun, 3 Sept, he wrote – "WAR DECLARED 11am Sept 3"*

Peter enjoyed exploring his new neighbourhood – Horsell Common has hundreds of acres of ancient wooded heathland so it was an idyllic spot for the budding young biologist. His diary entries for September are a mix of blackberrying on the common and biking around but are overlaid with increasing anxiety about the progress of the war.

*Thurs, 7 Sept – "This afternoon I rode over to Pam's and we rode to the common again. Went for a walk along the canal this eve. No bombs yet. War progressing hard in Poland"*

*Sat, 9 Sept – "I wrote to mum this morning. Had a long ride and rode to Pam's went there again this aft and Dad had come. We went blackberrying and Pam made some jelly. The French claim to have advanced 8 miles. Poland is retreating in order"*

*Sun, 10 Sept* – "went for a ride on my bike this morn and cleaned out my newts. Pam came over this afternoon and we rode to Guildford it was a lovely time went for a walk this evening. I have done 95 miles down here"

*Sat, 16 Sept* – "the Germans are but a few miles from Warsaw and have covered a great deal of land. Russia has now crossed the Polish frontier. 1000s of leaflets have been dropped over Germany"

*Wed, 27 Sept* – "I went over to Pam's this aft to do some gardening and after we went conkering. This eve I went for a lovely walk over the Golf Links. Warsaw has fallen and Poland is defeated"

*Sat, 30 Sept* – "Pam and I left at 9am this morn (to go to London) but when we reached Byfleet I had to go back for Pam's gas mask and arrived home (London) about 12 noon. We had Dinner at Grandma's and then Dad went down and fetched Mum. We all did some shopping in Putney this evening"

*Sun, 1 Oct* – "I completely blacked out the front room for Dad. I went for a ride on the common this aft and then Gran came to tea we had a tiny birthday cake for Dad's birthday next Sunday"

By October, both Peter and Pam were fed up with the places where they were billeted so they decided to return to live at home and to take the 30-minute train journey to school in Woking every day. They enjoyed being back with their grandmother and Percy during the period of the Phoney War, which Peter described as " all very odd".

*Thurs, 12 Oct – "Dad came down this afternoon and he brought me home, it is fine being back again. We had a lovely tea at Grandma's"* And he carries on visiting the zoo – *" I took a big carrier of acorns and a carrier of food for the animals. Not a soul there. We had a lovely time"*

But his diary entries are now interspersed with more news about the war:

*Sat, 14 Oct – "THE WAR. The Courageous and Royal Oak have been sunk by U-boats. About 20 U-boats have been accounted for however. The French have advanced very little"*

*Wed, 18 Oct – "did more homework this morn. I am doing a painting of a farm. I have decided to drop German"*

*Thurs, 19 Oct – "I have nearly got a complete set of "animals of the countryside" [these were cigarette cards made by John Player and Sons that were included in packets of cigarettes] I need 3 more"*

*Wed, 25 Oct – "THE WAR. There have been 2 or 3 raids on Scotland on Scarpa Flow and the other on Forth Bridge. No damage done 4 planes brought down"*

*Sun, 29 Oct – "I wore my long trousers for the first time today. Dad came and brought lots of games and things"*

Then, in November, he got ill with shingles and was bedbound for much of the month. "I have plenty of books but I don't like being in bed." He wrote lots of letters to "mum and Dad and Uncle Albert, Auntie Susie and Auntie Dolly, Auntie Ethel". Pam collected work for him from school and told him that pupils were already getting ready for Christmas. Peter wrote: "We are going to make a lot of coat hangers for Christmas presents." He carried on doing school work, going for walks, making coat hangers and bird watching.

> Wed, 22 Nov – "I went for a ride along the canal bank saw king-fisher, many long-tailed tits and a cock pheasant a few feet away"

> Wed, 13 Dec – "Russia has marched into Finland some weeks ago but Finns are holding out?"

Christmas comes but his biggest excitement was seeing a large bird foot-print in the snow: "6 inches by 5 inches, think it must be a heron. Went on to common and they were trying to catch a swan – saw rabbit track".

In 1940 he started a new diary just for his nature observations and wrote on the front: "Nature Diary – if found please return to: Peter Jewell, 7 West Hill Road, Wandsworth, London SW18 [where the family now lived] Thank you!!"

Every day he recorded the birds he had seen, and whether they were eating the food he put out for them.

Christmas card painted by Peter for his mother, 1939

> Fri, 5 Jan – "Heard the starlings evening 'song' at

*Trafalgar Square this eve – wrote to zoo man about those footprints (birds)"*

His entries read like a country diary in south London, there's no mention of anything but his observations of the natural world around him. He takes real pleasure and joy in what he is seeing and from using the telescope he had received for his birthday.

*Tues, 9 Jan – "heard robin clearly at 7.30am when the bird chorus began"*

*Sat, 13 Jan – "I have put two rows of peanuts for the tits which come eagerly"*

*Sun, 14 Jan – "the peanuts fell from the gutter into a bush and it was interesting to watch the tits coming to it while there. Dad bought down a letter from the Zoo man saying that the footprints were from a heron"*

*Mon, 15 Jan – "put out fresh peanuts was surprised to see long-tailed tits feeding on scraps right outside the window. There is a pretty chaffinch about, its head and wing (Ord white) are ginger."*

*Tues, 16 Jan – "I have now fixed up a bird tray outside and put seed and scraps in it. Blackbirds, thrush, robin and tits come to it so far."*

*Sat, 20 Jan – "Pam has now acquired the wing of the heron – it is very lovely."*

In January he wrote about the birds "eating snow" and how he listened to the bird song:

> "I was listening to a great tit. He had two different songs I find it very muddling" and Peter is particularly interested in the bird species and their markings "a very pretty dove came here today it was a very pale fawn a little darker on the back and grey in tail, a dark mark on its neck. I called and he answered me once. It was very tame. I wrote to Animal Zoo mag about the heron"

He next started identifying trees from a book "I identified a type of juniper today" – "there is a line of small trees in the garden which the gardener calls spruce but the nearest to it in my book is juniper – the leaves v small in pairs"

> Fri, 26 Jan – "I got a reply from Animal Zoo mag my letter is under consideration for publication. Rain makes things look much more like Spring"

He also made a nesting box and fixed it up in a tree – spring comes and the "trees are in bloom", the birds are singing and on Thursday, 21 March, he is excited to write, "tits started nesting in box today just a little moss. Have found several flies in loft waking up after winter." He watched the tits making their nest "pulling out strands from the bean strings". He collected some frogs' spawn and noted "I have a blood worm in a jar" – "one wallflower is out and so is the almond tree".

> Fri, 29 March – "Many tadpoles still unhatched. There is an increase in material in our (nest) box. I got April's 'Animal and

*zoo' mag and my letter (see Jan 26) is printed. Went to Rich-*
*mond park pond dipping – unsuccessful as no insects yet but*
*got a woodlouse like creature. Heard and saw many jackdaws*
*I believe".*

Peter carried on noting everything he observed, even "I saw an ant out today" (1 April). He noted that the trees were more out and covered in "small caterpillars", and continued visiting the zoo. He continued walking and going to the parks and heard a woodpecker "laughing". In the bird box there was a lot of material and the tits had left a hole in one corner. The tadpoles had lost their gills and he heard the pigeons crying and saw a tame robin "which hopped on Dad's back once".

Meantime, the Phoney War was over and fighting between European nations started in earnest. The Germans invaded France and then the air-raids started on London, but despite this the family stayed for some time living in Wandsworth. They had a Morrison shelter – a big table-like construction made of steel – erected in their living room. The shelters were given to householders by the government to try to protect people from falling debris during air-raids. When an air-raid started, the whole family would hide under it together.

Peter described it as a very scary time: "I can remember being frightened, I can remember being frightened for grandma. You could hear the bombs dropping and so it was all pretty unpleasant."

Ivy was still in the mental hospital at Dartford, in east London, where there were many more air-raids than in Wandsworth. Peter recalled visiting his mother "on the Green Line coach, which had netting stuck on to the windows so that if a bomb shattered the glass it wouldn't fly all over your face. Whenever the air-raid siren went, the bus would stop and we would all leap out and run into the nearest shelter and wait until the bombs had fallen, near or far. When the all-clear sirens went we would get back into the bus and continue the journey."

Between 1941 and 1942, as he grew older, Peter took to cycling to see his mother in Dartford, biking from Wandsworth through Clapham and Denmark Hill and New Cross, across the whole of south London, about 23 miles. The visits were a distressing experience for both him and Pam. As Peter described it: "It was terrible, because first of all the mental home was like a prison. Stonehouse it was called, Stonehouse Mental Hospital.

"You can imagine what it was like – a ghastly, gaunt, stone building, with miserable furniture inside and she slept in a small ward. The visiting room had chairs scattered about and you'd get a cup of tea, not much else, of course it was wartime so there wasn't much to be had anyway."

Peter and Pam used to try and save some of their rations to take to her, perhaps something she might like to eat, but she would be very weepy and distressed. He described how they "tried to cheer her up but of course as the years went by there was absolutely nothing to talk about because she didn't read the papers or know anything, she hardly read any news".

Percy and Ivy before she became ill

Peter recalled how they'd sit in silence and then he'd say: "What did you have for breakfast, mum?", and she'd say: "A boiled egg today". He'd say: "Oh that was nice", and there would be another long silence. He often spoke in later life about how difficult it had been for everyone, as he wrote: "Family life doesn't depend on talking about things, it depends on doing, on daily events and these things weren't happening. So it was all absolutely hopeless. I cried in despair as I cycled home."

There was often talk of Ivy coming out, and once or twice she did come home for a week, but then felt depressed and awful, and couldn't cope and had to go back. Certainly, with modern drugs she would have coped, she would have been calmer and very elementary doctoring might have got her back into the family, but it wasn't available then.

At 15 Peter took his matriculation, got good marks and didn't know what to do next. Percy didn't think there was any point in Peter continuing in the sixth form because he himself had no concept of higher education. Peter wanted to study animals but didn't know how to go about doing this, and the school hadn't been able to help him. He recalled: "When I was about 14 there was a careers advisory panel at school and I went to this full of apprehension. I was really embarrassed when I had to admit that I liked going to the zoo and looking at animals because it didn't seem an appropriate thing to be doing. It didn't seem to have much potential and they said – oh well you ought to try and be a zoo keeper, or work on a farm – and that was the extent of the projection of my future education. Nil, in other words."

In 1940 a scheme came up for young boys to go and work on farms, and Peter was sent to Somerset to work on a farm where they had lovely north Devon red cattle. It was very basic – there was no electricity, only candlelight, so it was a strange experience for the young London school-boy. Peter was supposed to be learning about farming but the farmer had no idea of how to teach him anything, so Peter did what he could for about six months and then got fed up and went to stay with Auntie Susie and Auntie Dolly who were not so far away in Teignmouth.

In 1941 the air-raids got worse and Percy decided to find a house out of London, moving the family to Wix Hill in Ripley, Surrey. Peter went to work full-time on a local dairy farm, Wix Farm, and was there for about a year through to 1942. He didn't like it, however, because at first he wasn't allowed to be with the animals. His job was to run the dairy – he sterilised the milk in the cooler and collected the bottled milk which was sold directly to locals, and washed all the dirty bottles. Later he moved from the dairy to the cowsheds and became a milker – he milked the cows by hand and cleaned the sheds.

At the end of 1942 Percy moved back to West Hill Road and Peter left the farm and decided to return to London too. As he wrote: "I recognized the hopeless gap in my further education, and decided to go to Chelsea Polytechnic to study for my Higher School Certificate in intermediate science, which was the same as I would have done in the sixth form at school, to try and get back into learning."

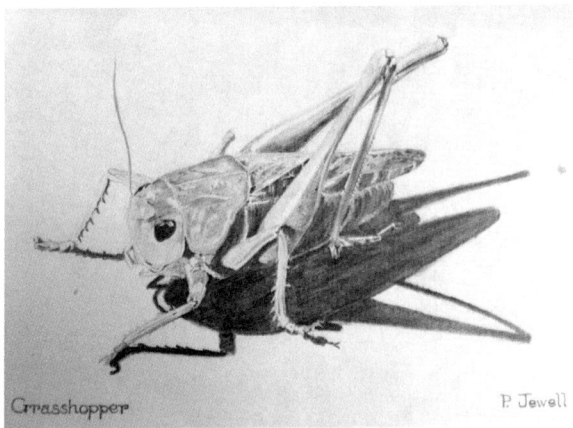

Grasshopper drawn by Peter when he was 15

# Into Africa: Juliet's wartime evacuation

# 3

After war broke out, Juliet's father Alan served in intelligence with the Royal Air Force volunteer reserve Bomber Command, and Barbara also worked there as a civilian for Operational Research, using photographic evidence to analyse the results of British raids. Children were being evacuated from London, so Alan, along with Juliet's grandmothers, decided that the safest and best thing for her and Francis would be for them to go and stay with their aunt Kathleen (Sheelah's sister) who lived in Rhodesia (now Zimbabwe).

Kathleen lived in a large house in the capital Salisbury (now Harare) with her husband William who was administrative head of the Transvaal Chamber of Mines. Kathleen had an eight-year-old son, Tristan, by her first marriage to Archie Russell who had died when Tristan was two. Kathleen was very fond of her niece Juliet (whom she called Judy) and nephew Francis and was glad to have this opportunity to look after them.

Kathleen was often away travelling with William and she wrote in a letter to Tristan at the time: "As you must know the war news is very bad and it might not be safe for Judy and Francis to stay in England so we are going to have them to come and stay with us. It will be great

fun having such a big family and you will be like a big brother to the two children. We must make them feel very much at home and comfy and share everything with them. They will feel strange at first, as you know they have no Mummy and now they will be away from their Daddy."

In her letter she says that she is also sending Tristan a little parcel with "a toad for you from Dad, a little boat for you from Mummy, and a little hippo made out of hippo tooth for you from Mummy". This was an indication of the delights to come for Juliet – exploring the African bush and discovering her lifelong interest in animals.

She adored her cousin Tristan who was just a year older than her, and they soon had the most idyllic and carefree time running barefoot in the African veldt – riding, playing with the dogs and going on adventures. It was here that her great passion for Africa began – she loved the heat, the huge African skies and the wide open spaces.

Juliet wrote about the preparations for getting ready to set sail: "My doll's house and other toys were taken to a children's home; Beau, our dog – the English setter, was put to sleep, and the nanny left." Ethel – the children's grandmother and Kathleen's mother – sailed to Cape Town with them.

They left Cheltenham on a train for Glasgow a day or so before 22 August 1940 – the day of Francis's fifth birthday – and Juliet describes how her father Alan came to see them off: "I remember him in the railway compartment where we had sleeping bunks with Granny. Father gave Granny two parcels for us, a small one which I assumed was for me and a bigger one that I assumed was for Francis as it was his birthday, but they were the other way around; the small one was a pocket watch and the bigger one was a navy blue zipped leather writing case which I kept until I was an adult. It had a little address book in it."

They took a night train to Glasgow and the next day they embarked on the RMS Arundel Castle, a Union Castle ocean liner and Royal Mail Ship which entered service in 1921 for the Union-Castle Line. The ship sailed from Glasgow to avoid the submarines and German bombs, and as far as Juliet remembered "nothing hit us on the voyage but there were many lifeboat practices. I felt seasick for most of the time and retched when Francis ate a green ice cream in front of me." When they crossed the equator Juliet was frightened by the ritualistic commotion of "throwing people in the swimming pool".

Granny Ethel and Beau

After arriving in Cape Town they took a train to Johannesburg, and Juliet remembered arriving at Kathleen and William's house, where the children shared one bedroom. Juliet, Tristan and Francis spent their time having lessons with a governess, Miss Wal-

Tristan and Juliet at Orange Grove

ters, and playing in the garden, "particularly egging on the bull terrier Billy to have fights with other dogs, whereupon we would turn a hose on them or throw pepper at them to stop the fights".

Soon after arriving Juliet developed a tubercular gland in her neck and had to have a nasty operation – the experience was so frightening that it gave her a lifelong phobia of hospitals and fear of anyone touching her neck. During the operation, tubes were put in the wound to drain it and they were changed every day causing her "agonising pain". The one good thing that happened, she said, was that her grandmother brought in a selection of teddy bears from a shop for her to choose from. "I chose a blue one with pink velvet feet and this much-loved teddy stayed with me until I gave it to my eldest daughter [Sarah, the author of this book]." Teddy, as he was called, went on to be one the family's favourite toys although the pink velvet paws had faded and the blue fur was light grey.

When Juliet came out of hospital she was sent to convalesce at Reed's Hotel at the seaside in Plettenberg Bay on the Cape with Francis, Tristan and Miss Walters. It was a happy time of "walking on the beach and catching fish from a little boat and going for rides in a little horse-driven cart". While the children played by the seaside, Kathleen and William moved to their beautiful newly bought house, Orange Grove, just outside Salisbury. And it was during this time that Kathleen and William's first baby, Alexander David Gemmill, was born, on 11 April 1941.

The only blot on the landscape was Miss Walters who was horrible to Juliet and overtly favoured Tristan. She was always thinking up "grossly unfair" punishments for her, and Juliet wrote in her memoirs: "Perhaps the worst was when she tied me up with a dog lead outside the back verandah for a morning. This was because she 'caught' me in the tool shed with the gardeners." What had happened was that Juliet had been in the toolshed with Tristan and the two dogs, hunting rats, "which was an approved activity", but unfortunately it was midday and the gong went for the gardeners to return to the shed with their tools before going off for lunch. Consequently, the children were trapped in there when the gardeners came in too – "Miss Walters happened to come along at the time and considered that I could commit no worse sin, and therefore I could not be trusted and would have to be tied up the next day."

After their seaside break, the children and Miss Walters returned to Salisbury to live at Orange Grove. There, the children slept upstairs with

Kathleen, Juliet's aunt

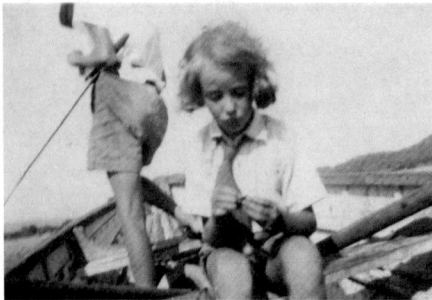
1941, Juliet and Tristan fishing

Miss Walters and Nurse. Downstairs they had their own day nursery in which they had lessons from Miss Walters and they each had a wooden toy-cupboard, which they had to keep tidy.

Juliet wrote that there was a large table in the middle of the room "where we had our lessons and also most of our meals – we used the back stairs and were allowed on the back verandah but not on the front verandah or up the front stairs or in the sitting room. Kathleen and William had their own suite of bedroom, dressing room and bathroom built on to the side of the house." On Sundays the children had lunch in the dining room but they weren't allowed in there at any other time.

It was at Orange Grove that Juliet developed her love of dogs – Tristan already had a small black Scottish terrier, called Ivanhoe, and it was her greatest desire to have a dog of her own too. "I expect I nagged about this a great deal because when Christmas 1941 arrived, I was prevented from going to the stables on Christmas Eve and then on Christmas Day I was given a black puppy that had been kept there overnight."

The puppy was a Rhodesian Ridgeback cross breed and Juliet called him Zimba after the dog in her favourite book at the time, *My Dog Simba* by Cherry Kearton. "I loved that dog more than anything in life and was terribly upset when I had to leave him to go to school, and even more so when I had to leave to come back to England. He was not allowed in the house and had a wooden kennel with a corrugated iron roof outside the kitchen. He had a sack stuffed with straw for a bed and I used to sit in the kennel with him."

With Zimba and Ivanhoe as their running mates, Tristan and Juliet spent many long hours playing together dressed in identical khaki shorts and shirts (with white ones on Sunday), as Juliet recalled: "The ten-acre garden was a paradise of freedom with infinite resources for childhood adventure and I neither needed nor had any friends other than Tristan."

In fact they were so adventurous that Juliet broke her left arm twice: "Tristan was always much more energetic than I was and he was the

Juliet and Zimba

leader in all games and exploits, while poor Francis was always left out, and we would run away from him, so he was left crying at the house."

The children were not supposed to go out of sight of the house but they always did. "There were tarantulas in the garden, which fascinated me and snakes that I was terrified of. I was told never to walk through dead leaves for fear of snakes and also I never slept with an arm hanging over the side of my bed, however hot it was, for fear of a snake lurking there."

Kathleen gave Juliet the option of learning either the piano or horse riding. She chose riding and the lessons were one of the highlights of her childhood: "We were driven once a week to a riding school owned by Mr Ashwin, a Boer War veteran. We rode round and round a small circle, I suppose for an hour, and we loved it, and Mr Ashwin claimed I had a 'good seat'." When she wasn't playing with the dogs or riding,

Juliet liked to watch the chickens and cows being fed. There were three or four cows that were milked every evening in a shed above the chicken runs and she was fascinated by everything to do with them, including the separation of the milk for cream and the churning for butter, which took place in an extension of the kitchen. However, there were some things she hated: "When the calves were shot in the stable and when the heifers were de-horned, which was an agonizingly painful process for them."

In due course both Tristan and Juliet were sent to school, he to a boys' school, St George's, and Juliet, for a while, to St Mary's convent in Salisbury. But she soon left there, and then she and Francis were sent as boarders to Chisipite School, about five miles out of town. This was a little prep school with a large garden. Juliet wrote that "everyone was very friendly but it was a rather rough place, there was a bucket in the middle of the floor at night for the children to pee in and it always overflowed. Also the sewage often overflowed outside the dormitory and smelt terrible. We had awful food and boiled milk with skin in it, which we had to drink. But I was happy at Chisip-ite, and I got a prize for 'good table manners' and a prize of some books for an English essay. There was bread and butter for break in the mornings which we roasted on the hot stones and there was a row of old camphor trees beside the front drive which provided shade and marvellous hiding places."

Some time after Juliet had been at Chisipite, it was decided the school should only be for girls and Francis had to leave. He was sent as a boarder to a small boys' prep school, King Edward's School, at the other side of town. In a letter to Doreen, Sheelah's sister, he wrote:

> "Dear Aunty Doreen, I hope you are having a nice time. I am going to school now and like it very much. I had my first home-works to do last week and like it very much.
> Love from Francis to aunty Doreen".

And in another letter he writes,

> "My dear Auntie Doreen, I hope you are well. I came first in my class, it is nice at school I am well and happy. I am working hard. Today is one of the boys birthday. Please will you send me some stamps. Yesterday we drew Humty-Dumty. Yesterday sister told us a story about birds nests. Lots of love from Francis."

Orange Grove painted by Kathleen

In December 1942, Kathleen and William had their second child, Mary; so there were now five children living at Orange Grove during the holidays. The livestock had also increased: there were large numbers of chickens and ducks; a few cows; and beehives to provide honey. The old tennis court next to the house had been replaced by a fine swimming pool in a well-kept walled garden and the whole establishment ran smoothly under Kathleen's energetic management, only she didn't have a lot of time for giving attention to the five children, and Francis and Juliet were often ill.

Juliet had caught tuberculosis soon after arriving in South Africa and Francis also developed a tubercular gland in his neck but luckily his was not as serious as the infection Juliet had suffered. He also had malaria and they both had chicken pox and had their tonsils and adenoids removed, which was a normal routine operation for children at that time. As Juliet wrote: "There were two doctors who always seemed to be visiting the house, Dr Rosen and his assistant Dr Richkin."

Juliet had diptheria at Chisipite school and was sent to an isolation hospital for two weeks, but the worst illness they both had was whooping cough, as Juliet described: "We were at Orange Grove when we caught it and it would have been dangerous for the babies so we were banned from the main house and had to stay in the rondavel guest house. We slept alone there at night and it was frightening, not only because it was dark and lonely but because we coughed all the time and Francis was often sick. An electric bell had been fixed up to call Nurse from the house if we needed her in the night but I don't think I ever rang it."

Juliet wrote in a letter to Alan that Francis was sick:

*"Dear Daddy, thank you so much for the air gram letter you sent me. I can read it thank you. I am sending you some stamps. Zimba is very well and big now. Yesterday Tristan and I had a swim in David's paddling pool. We have just broken up. Before we broke up we had a lovely concert. I won a prize for table manners. In class I came fourth out of seven. Francis has been sick but he is better now. It rained this morning but not much. With lots of love and kisses from Juliet."*

Then, in October 1943, when Juliet was at school, another terrible tragedy happened. She was having supper with the rest of the boarders at Chisipite, and remembered "sitting at the long table which was just inside the front door of the school and the office, when I heard the phone go. I felt sure the phone call was for me, and so it was." After supper Juliet was called into

Kathleen and William on a bush trip

the office by Mrs Anderson, the headmistress, who told her that Francis was very ill and was in hospital. "She said that as I would feel very worried about this I should come up to her house and spend the night with her. This I did and was put in a bed on her verandah. I didn't sleep well and in the night a cat came and lay on the bed and gave birth to kittens."

In the morning Mrs Anderson woke Juliet and told her that Francis had died and that she could go home to Orange Grove for a few days and take a friend with her. Juliet chose her best friend Valentine Barker and they went back together to Orange Grove that day: "It was all very strange and it was the first time I had ever had a friend at home and I felt it was very important that I look after her well. When we got there I found that everything to do with Francis had gone from the house and no one mentioned him."

Kathleen was not there at first, as she had been away on a bush trip with William but had been sent a radio message to return. Juliet spent a couple of days with Valentine waiting for Kathleen to come back. But there was little consolation when she did return and Juliet remembered that she heard Kathleen ask Nurse whether she had been very upset "and Nurse replied: 'No she doesn't seem at all worried, but just plays as usual

Francis and his toy dog

with her friend.' I felt this was unfair as I was trying my best to behave normally and look after Valentine."

Francis had been taken swimming by the nanny in the river when Kathleen was away, which she should never have done, and he caught polio and became fatally ill. For Juliet it was a traumatic second family tragedy – she had now lost her mother and her brother. Francis was only eight and Juliet was ten. She always felt guilty about Francis's death, and said she was haunted by the fact that the last words she remembered saying to him were "go away I don't want to play with you". Natural words for a child who loved playing with her older cousin and didn't want her little brother interfering, but it was a lifelong burden for her: "I never did feel any great sorrow at Francis's death, but for many years I had an overwhelming feeling of guilt that I had been horrible to him, and I don't think I have ever got over that guilt. I returned to school, everything returned to normal, and Francis went out of my life."

The next year, 1944, the whole family went on a "magical seaside holiday to the Cape" at Christmas – the long school holiday in southern Africa. Tristan and Juliet, David (aged three and a half) and Mary (aged two) and the governess went on the three-day train journey to Port Alfred, on the coast near Grahamstown. Kathleen, who was about five months pregnant with her daughter Josephine, and William travelled by plane. For Juliet this was a "truly wonderful holiday" and she remembered almost all their activities, particularly a dog and her puppies: "When we arrived at the house this bedraggled stray dog was lurking in a shed in the garden; we made friends with her and after a few days she caught hold of Tristan by his shorts and dragged him with her mouth into the shed where we found the litter of her puppies, which we of course immediately adored and fed with scraps from the kitchen from then on."

The children also caught small turtles on a fishing line and kept them in a water tank at the back of the house, and fed them on mussels but "all the water went putrid and the whole lot had to be thrown out". On the dunes they found three small tortoises (for Juliet, Tristan and David) and they took them back to Orange Grove in the train in a shoe box, in which Juliet had cut out some windows.

This was Juliet's first taste of the seaside: "There was a wonderful long sandy beach covered with shells and almost empty of people." The children were not allowed to swim in the sea because of the fear of sharks but they collected shells and Juliet found a Venus ear (abalone) shell and "stuck little shells round it as an ash tray, and it was sent off by post to my father in England. I saw it in the house when I arrived there."

They were sad when the wonderful holiday ended, but also "glad to be going home" and excited about the journey: "The compartments in the trains were wonderful little rooms with beds and basins with brass taps and all sorts of elaborate fixings and lights." On the three-day journey the train stopped at Kimberley and they all got off for a walk to a fruit and vegetable market where the governess bought a watermelon, which they all ate. "When we got home we put the tortoises in the swimming pool garden and they lived there for many years, but finally disappeared."

After the holiday, it was back to boarding school at Chisipite. About this time Tristan went on one or two bush trips with Kathleen and William, but Juliet wasn't allowed to go, being a girl and too young. But then, as a special treat, because she was going back to England she was allowed to join one. "I was enormously excited and I enjoyed this trip more than anything else I had ever done – it was the real high point of my childhood. Later I found the map I had drawn of the itinerary, which I had sent to my father in England."

Alan's communications with his daughter while she was in Rhodesia were infrequent and he had even less contact with Ethel, Juliet's grandmother. As the end of the war approached, Ethel wrote a rather ominous letter to Alan from her home in Cheltenham.

"My Dear Alan, it is a very long time since I have had any news of you. I hope you and Barbara are well also your mother. I would be pleased to hear what your plans are about Judy and if you are planning to send her to school if you have her home soon. She writes to me sometimes and seems to have done very well at Chisipite. I expect you are counting the days to get back to civilian life and freedom, are you in an early category? Do you find time to do any painting? With kind regards to Barbara and your mother, Yours affectionately, Ethel M Archer".

Juliet had always known that she would have to leave Orange Grove to go back to England, but hadn't given it much thought. In the event, it was a terrible wrench to leave the home and family she loved in Africa. Kathleen later told Juliet that she would have liked to adopt her but Alan had decided he wanted his daughter back. In 1946, when she was 12, he decided it was safe for her to return. Juliet wrote to him saying:

"My dear Daddy, thank you so very much for the letter you sent me, which I received yesterday. I cannot tell you how much I am *longing to see you and mummy [Barbara] again. It will be such fun going to England again, after I have not seen beautiful England for so long. A small house in the country with a little garden and perhaps a small dog of my own, that is if I am not asking for too much, is just what I am longing for. All my love and kisses your loving daughter Juliet."*

Preparations were made for Juliet's return trip and Kathleen chose a trunk, which she packed with clothes, toys and books, and some tinned foods for Alan and Barbara. She also bought Juliet warm clothes and a brown tweed coat.

The journey back to England involved a three-day train journey to Cape Town from where Juliet was to go by ship back to Southampton. On the train journey she was accompanied by a woman who Kathleen had arranged to look after her. The day arrived and in the evening Juliet went to the station with Kathleen and William, and met the woman on the train. "Kathleen was crying, but I just felt overwhelmed with it all. The train journey was long and hot, and I was sick several times in the basin in the compartment, which blocked it up, so I wasn't very popular with my new companion."

Then they arrived at the ship, the Carnarvon Castle, a Union-Castle Line ship that had been converted to a troop ship and was carrying WRNS from Cape Town back to England, as well as a few private passengers. Sadly, there was an unpleasant surprise waiting for Juliet: "I suppose I already knew, but I hadn't thought about it much, that the person who Kathleen had employed to take me back to England was our old governess, Miss Walters, perhaps the only person in my life so far who I had hated. So it wasn't a happy trip."

It was a harsh start to Juliet's new life in England.

# Cold porridge and sea swimming: Juliet's school days and Jacobean home life

# 4

The Carnarvon Castle arrived at Southampton on 5 April 1946. It was cold and damp and grey in England, unlike anything that Juliet could remember and was a huge culture shock. She was very homesick for Orange Grove and her family in Africa but was sent as a boarder to Runton Hill School in West Runton, Norfolk, where the headmistress, Janet Vernon-Harcourt (known as JVH), was a cousin of her father. Julia Allen was a fellow boarder and became one of Juliet's lifelong friends. She recalls that "West Runton was a cold place, cold even for those who had lived in England during the War. What must it have been like for someone returning from Rhodesia? In the winter of 1946 snow came up to the tops of the hedges and the school had no central heating. We piled our bedside mats on top of us to keep warm. Our sponges (kept in fishnets hung beside our beds) were often frozen by morning and there would be frost patterns inside the dormitory windows. Most of us had chilblains, which itched and split on hands and feet."

Rationing was still in place and the food was very basic. Lumpy breakfast porridge was cooked overnight "in a haybox" and Julia remembers that the first time some bananas were brought to the school "they came up the drive on a trolley during a lesson and we all surged to the window to see these amazing fruit, but our classroom happened to be next to JVH's study and she stormed in and issued order punishment marks all round". The academic record of the school was not highly acclaimed and, as Julia said, "one wonders how young newly graduated teachers were recruited to such a bleak, out-of-the-way place – it's impossible now for me to assess the quality of teaching, but the school had quite a good record of Oxbridge entries". Religion, which was taught by JVH, was C of E and seemed founded on "inculcating a sense of guilt".

Runton Hall is described in the book *Terms & Conditions: Life in Girls' Boarding Schools, 1939-1979*, where one former pupil, Patricia Bergqvist, recalls: "A speciality of Miss Vernon-Harcourt was demystifying the Miracles – a stout disciplinarian with grey hair in a bun – she told us that Lazarus wasn't really dead; that there simply were enough loaves and fishes to go round at the picnic; and that Jesus walking on water was an optical illusion. All their lives, the girls who were told these things by their headmistress have been as unimpressed by New Testament magic as a too-clever boy watching a conjuror." Juliet was an ardent atheist her whole life and detested the hypocrisy of the church and "god-botherers" as she always called the clergy.

Not all the sciences were taught and for A-levels Juliet and Julia were sent to nearby Gresham's boys' school to learn chemistry and physics, where they made a few friends but were also teased. One of their classmates in physics was Colin Leakey, the son of Louis Leakey the paleoanthropologist, and he became a lifelong friend.

One day when Juliet was sitting on the bus going there, a couple of boys sitting behind cut her pigtails off, which she always remembered as quite a traumatic experience. Games played at Runton Hall were lacrosse, netball, rounders and tennis, but according to Julia the girls were "usually beaten by beefy amazons from Cromer or Norwich high schools". The games field, at the top of the windswept cliff, could be "very, very cold". Gym was usually done outside "in blue aertex shirts and blue school knickers (changed once a week), but there was a gym hut in a field – by the end of my time I could climb a rope using my hands and arms only. There was an annual house relay race up Beeston Bump and back."

Juliet and her bicycle

On Sundays, the girls were allowed to bicycle (two or more together) to a church of their choice, and Julia remembers her and Juliet bringing frogs back in their school hats for dissection after one church trip. They bought a tortoise, named Wellington, from the Army & Navy Stores but he didn't live long: "We buried him, intending to dig him up when he had become a skeleton, but could not find his grave."

In the summer term, the girls would bath in the sea. They would undress on the pebbly beach and "at the blast of a whistle, dash in". Julia recalls that "you had to be immersed by a second whistle blast and you were not supposed to go out of your depth, and when a whistle was blown you had to demonstrate you could stand by raising both hands. Swimming was not taught, you just did your own thing in the water."

Juliet used to say that in rough seas the girls were roped together so that they wouldn't get dragged out by the currents. Once a shark was washed up on the beach and Julia and Juliet tried to pull out its teeth to make a necklace, "but they were not to be budged". Once each summer they also had Blakeney Day, when the girls were driven in coaches to Blakeney and taken in boats to Blakeney Point. "We had to walk over the shingle to the picnic place, being dive-bombed by terns on the way, and at some point there was a swim. Sunscreen had not been invented, and we would return burnt by sun and wind."

Julia also found some references in her father's diary to Juliet:

*Mon, 3 January 1949 – Welwyn*
*Jules's friend, Juliet Clutton-Brock, has arrived – rather nice.*

*Mon, 5 Sept 1949 – Welwyn*
*Jules back from York and brought her school friend Juliet Clutton-Brock who is a nice sensible child and one day is going to be very attractive as well. We made cider cup and all got jolly. The elder girls slept out in the warm moonlight rather by my instigation.*

*Tues, 7 Jan 1950 – Welwyn*
*The dear girls went back to school today in good heart. After we had seen them off we went to see Alan Clutton-Brock's paintings*

A landscape by Alan Clutton-Brock

*in Bond Street. He's the father of Jules's best friend and art critic of the "Times". He paints nice scenes of village houses and landscape in Suffolk.*

Juliet's little sister Eleanor

During the holidays, Juliet went to Chastleton House where Alan, Barbara and Eleanor were living. There, she enjoyed learning the history of the house, which was full of ancestral relics and artfacts – many of the contents that were listed in the 1633 inventory of the house remained in situ. The house had been built by Walter Jones, and his son Henry Jones married Anne Fettiplace and they had 13 children – the fireplace in the Fettiplace room is engraved with her coat of arms to commemorate their marriage. Henry's son, Arthur Jones, was the "Cavalier" who hid in a secret space in the Cavalier room to escape Cromwell's soldiers after the Battle of Worcester in 1651. Arthur's wife, Sarah, gave laudanum to Cromwell's soldiers and once they were asleep helped Arthur escape on one of the soldier's horses. The house was inherited by direct descendants until 1828 when the ownership passed to a Shropshire cousin – John Henry Whitmore who was married to Dorothy Clutton. Dorothy and John Whitmore had seven children and their son Walter Whitmore became a gamesman and inventor. In 1865 The Field published his version of the rules of croquet – and in 1868 the first croquet championships were held at Evesham and won by him.

A 1819 portrait of John Henry Whitmore, when he was 21. He died on 5 March 1854, aged 56

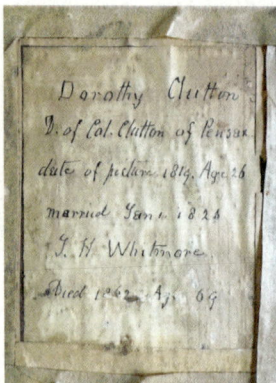

Portrait of Dorothy Clutton, 1819. Written on the back: daughter of Col. Clutton of Pensax. Age 26, married JH Whitmore 1821. Died 1862, aged 69

The Long Gallery, Chastleton

Juliet with her old school bicycle in the cellars of Chastleton

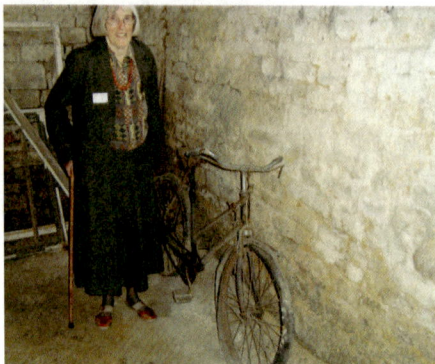

Built in 1604 and never dusted since

In 1954, Alan became the last remaining relative of the Clutton family to inherit the house. After his death in 1976, Barbara continued living there until 1991 when she sold the house to the National Heritage Memorial Fund, which passed it on to the National Trust. It was the first time that the house had been on the market in its 400-year history.

The National Trust (NT) made a deliberate decision to keep its shabby gentility, and Angus Stirling, director general of the NT, wrote in a letter to The Independent in 1991 that "it would be hard to conceive of a house where it is more necessary to avoid standardised practice than Chastleton. We shall do everything we can to respect and maintain the appearance of this magical place, inside and out, as it has come to us, and avoid 'tasteful upgrading' ".

By the time the house was sold, many of the rooms were decrepid and the roof was leaking badly, but the house had always had an air of gentle neglect and the undisturbed soot of four centuries coated the kitchen ceiling – legend had it that if the soot was ever cleaned off good luck would desert the family. The house holds many treasures such as the Juxon Bible in the library, which is said to have been used by Bishop Juxon at the execution of Charles I in 1649.

Juliet enjoyed the holidays at Chastleton but it was quite a lonely time as Alan and Barbara were busy showing visitors around and her sister Eleanor was much younger than her. She enjoyed running about in the Long Gallery – a most beautiful room at the top of the house, which was built for exercising in and has the longest barrel-vaulted ceiling in the land.

Juliet also loved playing in the garden, which had a huge topiary with hedges cut into shapes of a cakestand, cat, teapot, sheep, chicken, horse, squirrel, ship in full sail, peacock and crown. A few years before she died, Juliet went back to Chastleton and was amazed to see that her old school bicycle was still in the basement.

# Farming, fishing and physiology: Peter's student days

# 5

Peter enjoyed his time at Chelsea Polytechnic and in his last year he joined the Communist Party, along with Pam and their friend Alan Ness. He liked going to student meetings and getting into debates on communism and socialism. He also joined the Association of Scientific Workers while studying zoology, botany, geology and chemistry. At this time, he thought about doing a degree in zoology but he was discouraged by his lecturer (despite being top in his class) because of the poor job opportunities it offered. So instead he decided to do a degree in agriculture.

Peter sat for a scholarship exam for Reading University and was awarded £80 per year. Around that time, he was told he should try for medicine and had an interview at Queen Mary University of London. But as he already had the Reading scholarship and wanted to help his father financially he decided to go there. He started at Reading in September 1943 – it was a three-year course but because of the war they did an extra fourth term during the summer. The course he had already done at Chelsea Polytechnic was equivalent to the first year so he went straight into year two of the agriculture course. He lived in Wantage Hall and there he met Sidney Holt who was reading Zoology, Botany and Chemistry, who became a lifelong friend and they shared a room together.

Sidney described their time at Reading: "I spent days walking with Peter in the meadows as he tried to learn how to name a great variety of grass species. He and I went off to the Norfolk Broads sailing, with a couple of girls from the Uni. We both got into student politics – he became President of the Students' Union, I became vice-president, in charge of sports, games and societies. We were both Communists, and at the post-war general election Peter went to Wandsworth, supporting the Communist Party candidate. We carried a soap box one Saturday morning and he harangued the people at the market. My role was to heckle him loudly in order to draw a crowd."

Sidney and Peter both enjoyed acting and they got involved in performing in Shakespeare's Henry IV Part I at Reading. Sidney recalled that Peter had one line "I saw young Harry with his beaver on", and he couldn't decide where the emphasis should be. "We spent much time discussing whether it should be on Harry, saw, beaver, on, or I. I helped him practise. I was a herald, playing my jazz cornet as a bugle – except when it came to the actual performance I had make-up on my lips and could only blow raspberries."

Peter spent the summer vacations of 1943-45 working on farms and avoided call up because he was an agricultural student. He later wrote, "I regretted not being called up – I missed out on the experience of comradeship of war." He graduated in Easter 1945 but had not enjoyed his time at Reading. The course wasn't challenging intellectually and it was very technical, and he knew that he didn't want to become a farmer.

In the early summer of 1945, Peter finished at Reading. He had always enjoyed fishing and was curious to find out more about deep sea trawling so he wrote to the Boston Ice Fishing Company at Hull,

Peter in his Cambridge days

which offered him a role as a deckhand. He joined a boat leaving Fleetwood, in Lancashire, for Iceland, but was worried about seasickness. He had been given potassium bromide, a sedative, at the chemist's but was sick every day and he felt terrible, losing half a stone in weight.

The boat was fishing for hake and Peter's job was to gut the fish and then throw them into the hold where they were put on ice. Peter wrote an article about the experience for the Reading University magazine: "The moment of real excitement came when, 400 fathoms of cable having been wound in, there were some 50 fathoms to come. Then speculation as to the catch ran high. The gannets, too, were watching expectantly, circling excitedly above us, yellow throats outstretched, eyes piercing deep into the ocean, until suddenly they would fold their wings and dive with unerring precision into the sea."

Then the net came up and it was all hands on deck. "The nets were manhandled on board: using each lurch of the ship to help us with the tug, and hanging on with grim determination as the side dipped below the surface and the sea poured over us." The bag of fish – hake, ling, halibut and bream, was heaved by winch up on to the deck, "a sharp tug on one of those infallible seaman's knots and the bag burst open pouring its

Peter at Cambridge

contents into the deck compounds." On one occasion five hundred stone of fish lay on deck "not a writing mass as one might expect, but a pile of little silver corpses, killed by the great pressure in the net and now corpulent with air". Then work began on the catch. Peter was instructed: "Cut 'em up the middle, put the livers in them baskets, whip out the guts and don't leave no bit in!" Then the fish were washed and packed in ice below deck. It was very hard work – 18 hours on deck, and then between midnight and dawn every man had to do a two-three hour watch. "None of us ever got more than two hours' sleep at a stretch," Peter recalled.

Inside the cabin it was hot and smelly, and a coal stove added to the "fug" making the place at times unbearable. However the men were great company for whom, Peter wrote, "one can have nothing but admiration". They often asked him: "What do you think to fishing now, mate?," and Peter said he'd reply: "Not much." They'd respond: "No, it's a dog's life, mate, you take my tip and stick to farmin'."

That summer he was deeply upset because his mother, Ivy, had undergone a frontal lobotomy – a surgical procedure during which certain nerves and pathways to the brain are severed (think Jack Nicholson in *One Flew Over the Cuckoo's Nest*). The idea of the lobotomy was to help patients with severe anxiety and depression by cutting the connections between the frontal lobes and the rest of the brain. But after her operation Ivy became withdrawn and non-communicative, and was still depressed, which Peter found disturbing.

A lobotomy was a very crude and brutal operation, which was nicknamed the ice-pick lobotomy and first performed in 1935 by the Portuguese neurologist Egas Moniz, and then in America in 1936 by psychiatrist Walter Freeman. It was written about in a National Public Radio article: "As those who watched the procedure described it, a patient would be rendered unconscious by electroshock. Freeman would then take a sharp ice pick-like instrument, insert it above the patient's eyeball through the orbit of the eye, into the frontal lobes of the brain, moving the instrument back and forth. Then he would do the same thing on the other side of the face." From the early 1940s, it began to be seen as a miracle cure in the UK, where surgeons performed proportionately more lobotomies than even in the US. But from the mid-1950s, it rapidly fell out of favour, partly because of poor results and partly because of the introduction of the first wave of effective psychiatric drugs.

Once Peter had completed his fishing trip, he wanted to come back to London to help support his mother and to let Pam get on with studying medicine at St George's Hospital, so he returned temporarily to the family home at West Hill Road.

Having graduated from Reading in 1945 with a first-class degree, Peter had three choices – to go to London University and study genetics under JBS Haldane, to Edinburgh University to study physiology under Professor de Burgh Daly or to Cambridge and study physiology under ED Adrian (later Lord Adrian). He chose Cambridge "because it was the most prestigious" and did a two-year BA in physiology. He had rooms in St John's College and became friends with Keith Westlake – who was a member of the Green Shirts and very left-wing. He was bright but troubled and later committed suicide because, as Peter said, he was under "too much pressure". Another of Peter's friends, Carl Schwarz, also committed suicide – they had met at Chelsea Polytechnic and in 1946 Peter, Carl and Alan Ness went to the first International Youth Rally for Peace and Socialism, which was held in Budapest. The deaths of his friends deeply affected Peter and contributed to his latent feelings of anxiety and depression.

It was during his time at Cambridge that Peter started having anxiety problems and became increasingly unsettled. In Easter 1947 he was living in digs in All Saints Passage, Cambridge. The landlady Miss Young objected to Peter bringing a girl home at 4pm for tea. Peter reported this to his tutor, Colin Bertram, who had words with Miss Young and this led to her "hating him".

He wanted to stay after term finished to do work during the Easter of 1947 for the exams in May. He moved to new digs but couldn't sleep at night. He was "shaking with fear in bed and felt very agitated and depressed". He couldn't work and felt intensely anxious, so a friend suggested they go and build sandbag barricades to stop the floods (1947 was a severe winter for floods). As Peter recalled: "This was a very good thing to do and the anxiety passed."

When Peter started his PhD at Cambridge in October 1947, Sidney introduced him to Philip Thomas and the three of them became inseparable. Philip was an old school friend (from Haberdashers') of Sidney's and was at Emmanuel College. Sidney described how Phil was also a communist and "we started our proclamations with grafitti on the dance hall wall at Cricklewood: 'Opium for the masses!' "

Eventually Peter and Phil left the communist party but Sidney, who later became a director of the Food and Agriculture Organisation of the

UN based in Rome, stayed connected to some extent. But, as he pointed out: "Eventually as a UN staff member living in Italy, I could not belong to a political party and be active. The difference was, I was in a country where more than a third of the population voted communist, and with party membership at one million. Also, of the three of us, I was actually the only one with an entirely working class background."

Sidney recalled how Peter's fishing trip in 1945 had a profound impact on him: "One thing Peter did that affected my life was go on a trawler voyage from Fleetwood to Iceland and back. I have somewhere the letter he wrote me during that. He had an awful time, weatherwise, but it was not enough to stop me getting into fisheries research, although the account of his trip nearly put me off! I was studying biology and wanted to be a vet but my parents couldn't afford the seven-year

Phil, Sid and Peter – the three inseparable friends

training. My professor at Reading had worked in Canada on fish and he suggested I do fisheries research when I began my final honours year."

Sidney went on to become one of the most influential marine biologists of the 20th century, a lifelong campaigner against commercial whaling and a scientific adviser to Greenpeace.

Peter's PhD at Cambridge was on the physiology of the dog and he wrote his thesis on *The blood supply to the hypothalamus of the dog.* He read the works of Ivan Pavlov and was interested in the work of EB Verney who was working with dogs and studying the osmotic pressure of body fluids with antidiuretic hormones. Verney became Peter's supervisor and he wanted to find out what part of the brain of dogs responded to osmotic pressure circulating in the blood. They took a loop of the artery out of the neck so it made it easier for injections. Peter hated doing the research on dogs because of the suffering it caused but he completed his PhD and graduated from Cambridge in 1951.

Peter's registration document allowing him to work on the fishing trawler

Peter at Reading University

# From Vet school to the Zoo: Peter's early career and marriage to Juliet

# 6

P eter now had a degree in agriculture from Reading, a degree in physiology from Cambridge and a PhD from Cambridge, so he started applying for jobs. In 1951 he was appointed lecturer in pharmacology at the Royal Veterinary College, University of London in Camden Town under Professor EC Amoroso (Amo). Peter actually didn't want to pursue a career in pharmacology but Amo had just created a lectureship in pharmacology for vets and Peter wanted to return to London and therefore took the job. He had to write lectures in pharmacology and do practical exercises – three lectures a week per term – that was 30 lectures per term. He did two terms of lectures and then spent the rest of the year marking exams. Peter "hated it"; the work wasn't interesting and he had an aversion to learning and lecturing about drugs because of the horrific experiences he'd had with his mother.

Peter's job was stressful but his home life was difficult too. He tried to be a peacemaker between his mother and grandmother – who always quarrelled when his mother came home for visits – and his father, who lived at home intermittently. His father eventually moved out to live with his girlfriend, Diana Bishop, at 28 Girdwood Road, Southfields.

Peter, photo by Ramsey and Muspratt

Pam was doing her house job and living in the hospital and at West Hill Road – but Peter felt increasingly unable to cope with the situation at home. He had a persistent sore throat and became so ill that his friends Alan and Christian Ness said that he should go and live with them to try and recover. Alan was a lecturer at University College London in dental physiology. Christian Ness was the partner in her father's firm of architects, Colcutt and Hamp, and she and Alan lived in a flat in Wigmore Street that belonged to the firm. The move to live with the Nesses was a good one. Peter recalled: "I was looked after by them away from the corrosive home atmosphere – but then I was struck down with intense anxiety again. I woke up and couldn't get up I was so anxious." He thought it was depression and the doctor gave him amytal tablets, a barbiturate sedative, and he remained on barbiturates for another 20 years to help him sleep at night.

Despite his anxiety, Peter struggled on, continuing to work at the Royal Veterinary College with the help of the sedatives, but he said he felt "drugged day after day". He didn't dare admit he was mentally ill as he didn't want to go into a home like Stone House where his mother had lived. He later wrote: "I should have gone to hospital and been given appropriate drug and psychiatric treatment, but I had to cope on my own."

After all the trials and tribulations, Peter's life was about to take a turn for the better, thanks to a chance meeting. In June 1953, he met Juliet as they were getting on a bus at Charing Cross to go on an archaeological field trip to Piltdown in Sussex, arranged by the Institute of Archaeology.

Alan and Christian Ness – Peter and Juliet's closest friends

Juliet said that after sitting next to Peter on the bus, she went home and told her best friend and flatmate, Sarah Cadbury, that she had met the man she was going to marry.

Later, Peter told Alan that he liked Juliet because she was good company and they were "both interested in archaeology and animals". He described her as a "very attractive young woman – despite wearing her aunt's cast-off clothing". Shortly after their first meeting however Juliet went off to work on an excavation in Chios, and they didn't see each other for a year. Peter kept in touch with her while she was away and, meanwhile, the Nesses took a house at 37 Newton Road, in Bayswater, west London, and offered Peter the basement flat.

While Juliet was in Chios, Peter became increasingly interested in archaeology and he met Sonia Chadwick at an excavation at Mawgan Porth – a Saxon Dark Age site in Cornwall. She was a young, attractive archaeologist and they started going out, however their relationship didn't last and when Juliet returned from Chios she started going out with Peter. He described Juliet as "kind, sympathetic and supportive and I felt confident

Peter on a dig and, below, working on artefacts

with her – we got on well together and there was no threat of me becoming depressed. We enjoyed going to the opera and theatre together."

In 1956 Peter went to Sweden to join his friend Bengt Anderson so Juliet moved into Peter's flat with her school friend Sarah Cadbury. Bengt was a friend from the Royal Veterinary College and Peter stayed in Sweden for six months doing more experiments on goats and dogs. He was experimenting on the brain but didn't like doing it – the work involved stimulating different parts of the hypothalamus and looking at how goats drank. Peter was pushing needles into the animal's brains and using an electric current to stimulate the hypothalamus. By the end of six months he so hated doing the experiments that after leaving Sweden he decided to stop them.

By now he knew that he wanted to look at animals in their natural environment and not to work in a laboratory. In 1957 Peter moved to the animal husbandry department at the Royal Veterinary College, where he worked on animal nutrition. He became a lecturer in animal husbandry and the domestication of

Juliet in 1957

animals, and this was when his interest in large and small mammals took off.

His first introduction to studying British wild mammals was on a trapping expedition on Dartmoor with Ian Linn, an enthusiastic young Scotsman who was a lecturer at Exeter University. They were carrying out a small-mammal survey for the Nature Conservancy. Peter followed this with further studies of bank voles and wood mice in forests near the Veterinary College Field Station at Potters Bar, in Hertfordshire.

In the summer of 1957, Peter and Juliet went on holiday to Orkney and the Shetland Islands, but Peter was concerned that his anxiety would return and paralyse him again. He was living in fear of his mental state. His sister had become engaged to a young doctor, Tom Pilkington, who worked at the same hospital as her. Before long, they were married, but Peter couldn't remember anything about the wedding because he was "so drugged at the time". Pam and Tom then moved in at West Hill Road with Ivy, now out of hospital, Ivy's mother and a friend, Miss Younger.

Peter's mental state gradually improved however, and he and Juliet started talking about living together. On 26 June 1958 they married at Chelsea Town Hall and went to live in the flat at the Nesses house at 37 Newton Road. Eighteen months later, their first daughter, Sarah, was born.

In May 1961 their second daughter, Vanessa Topsy, came along, and in July 1963 their third daughter, Rebecca Tamsin. Juliet always said she would have liked a fourth child – and a son – but that was not to be.

Peter and Juliet on their wedding day with Alan Ness in background

In 1960, after 10 years at the Royal Veterinary College, Peter became a research fellow at the Zoological Society of London in an exciting new laboratory that had been set up by Solly Zuckerman to look at the control of mammalian populations and to develop new projects that would form part of an integrated study of population dynamics and breeding biology in mammals. The laboratory secured funding from the Ford Foundation which Zuckerman had contacts with through a mutual interest in world population problems.

By basing the laboratory at London Zoo, Zuckerman's initial proposal argued, its researchers would be able to exploit the richness of the Zoological Society of London's collections and

Peter holding Sarah and Topsy, on holiday in Brittany

Peter at London Zoo in 1960 – back row, second from right

its breeding records, which dated back to 1828. Peter was appointed the senior investigator and funding was secured from the Wellcome Trust to house the laboratory in a new building – the Wellcome Institute of Comparative Physiology at Regent's Park next to the zoo.

It was an exciting fresh start for Peter, and in 1961 he began his ground-breaking series of studies of the population dynamics of small mammals on islands by looking at Soay sheep on St Kilda, in the Outer Hebrides. He was particularly interested in the Soay sheep, he wrote, because they were an "isolated feral population confined on the island and so presented an excellent opportunity to study populations fluctuations. They are also the most primitive of domestic sheep surviving in Europe, believed to be a Bronze Age survival and so there was an added interest from an archaeological point of view."

Peter's early training as a physiologist was invaluable here, and enabled him to combine experiment and observation. The work on the Soays involved marking lambs every year so that he could readily assess the age composition of the population. He wanted to study "the incidence of silent ovulation in the ewes and the proximate factors that bring the ewes into oestrus with such striking synchrony".

St Kilda offered a unique opportunity to study the role of rams because they were in such high numbers "of an order never maintained in commercial flocks – an experiment I propose to carry out is to castrate a high proportion of the males in one of the sub-populations and see how this affects the behaviour, longevity and reproductive activity in all the members of the home-range groups involved – such experimental interference with free-living populations of any wild mammal has rarely been carried out". In 1974 Peter published his research in his seminal book *Island Survivors: the ecology of the Soay sheep of St Kilda*.

Peter's research work also took him to the island of Skomer, off the coast of Pembrokeshire, where he looked at population density of field mice and voles, and began a new project: "I found the study of small mammals most rewarding being particularly interested in their annual reproductive cycle and population dynamic and I started the study of the Skomer vole and Skomer field mouse that was continued for many years."

Peter also made his own, considerable contribution to archaeology by inspiring the Experimental Earthwork project. At the 1958 meeting of the British Association for the Advancement of Science he proposed an experimental earthwork, with the idea of building a simple ditch and bank with objects placed within it, to be excavated and monitored in sections at intervals over many years. He was inspired by the work his hero, Charles Darwin, had done on the role of earthworms in the denudation of the land and the burial of buildings.

In 1959, a committee of archaeological pioneers was set up with Peter and Richard Atkinson, Ian Cornwall, Geoffrey Dimbleby, Bruce Proud-

Peter in later years posing as his hero Charles Darwin

foot and Paul Ashbee "to investigate by experiment the denudation and burial of archaeological structures".

In a subsequent report on the team's achievements, *The Experimental Earthwork Project 1960-1992*, M Bell, PJ Fowler and SW Hillson, wrote "what they were trying to do was, both in its thinking and in its interdisciplinarity, at least half a generation, perhaps even a full one, ahead of its time".

As they go on to say, "the idea of doing things by committee was very much in vogue in a positively socialist intellectual climate of a post-War society still innocently believing that 'things' could be improved, including society itself". The report continues: "We see here a reaching out into multi-disciplinarity, not just a recognition that Atkinson's archaeological approach, Cornwall's (1956, 1958) burgeoning knowledge of bones and soils, Dimbleby's journey from forestry to environmental science (1965) and Jewell's (1958) ecological sense could be applied together to History and Science; but also that the results of such research would be better History and Science. Indeed, surely here are seeds of something to be called interdisciplinary knowledge."

In 1960, the first earthwork, constructed under Peter's supervision, stood on Overton Down's chalk and it was decided to look in detail at the data acquired after 8, 16 and 32 year sections – in 1968, 1976 and 1992 – and finally a 64-year section. Peter wrote about the earthworks in his paper *The experimental earthwork on Overton Down, Wiltshire*: "The year 1958 saw the centenary of the publication of Charles Darwin's Origin of species. This great occasion was widely celebrated and inspired many of the papers presented at that year's meeting of the British Association for the advancement of science held in Glasgow. Juliet Clutton-Brock and I newly married attended the meeting and I was invited to talk at a joint session entitled the Darwin Centenary. I called my talk *Natural history and experiment in archaeology* (Jewell, 1958). In this talk I emphasised particularly Darwin's observations on earthworms and his speculations that objects would gradually sink into the soil through the action of earthworms.

"I felt this cried out for some experimental controls or contrived replication, that would help interpretation, and so in my talk I suggested that an experimental earth work should be built and studied to document the process of denudation and silting. It was an exhortation rather than a proposal but I thought it might win support as an apt celebration of Darwin's work. Following Darwin's example I thought the experiment

White rhino, photographed by Peter in the Serengeti

should be long-term, indeed as long as 100 years just as Darwin's chalk and cinder experiment had become when finally re-examined by Sir Arthur Keith in 1941."

Peter's original report became known as the *Basic Manual* and he continued to edit it, detailing the nature and implications of the earthwork. A further such earthwork was set up on acid-soil heathland at Morden Bog, Dorset, in 1963.

In 1997 Peter, along with Paul Ashbee, wrote a paper on *The Experimental Earthworks Re-visited*, and described how they had "laboured for so long at the design of the simple ditch and bank" and that they were "pleasantly surprised at the interest in precise aspects of the inherent changes of the buried materials". The next section through the Overton Down Earthwork, at 64 years, is planned to take place in 2024, by which time, they wrote, "further changes to structure and materials will have taken place, some of which are likely to have been, even today, unanticipated".

Aside from his archaeological interests, Peter was also developing his major interest in studying mammals. In 1962 he went on a three-month tour of East and Central Africa, visiting research institutes involved in wildlife studies. This led to the work that he became most passionate about – studying the management of large animals in game reserves and how they interacted with local people. He camped out in the Serengeti and loved the thrill of living in the bush with the wild African animals around him and learning about field work. He started in Uganda in the Queen Elizabeth National Park with a Cambridge graduate who was analysing the stomach contents of the hippopotamus and assessing the damage they were doing to their habitat. Then he went to Semliki to look at the Uganda kob and their mating and reproductive behaviour. This was followed by a trip to Murchison Falls where he saw the destruction caused by elephants. At Murchison he also saw black rhinoceros for the

Peter on a bush trip in the Serengeti

first time but failed to see any of the recently introduced white rhinoceros – which had come from the West Nile reserves where they were being poached on a massive scale. In his report Wild Life Research in East and Central Africa, Peter describes how 60 white rhino skeletons were found by the game warden but the skulls were not collected – although they would have been of enormous interest: "It was depressing to learn that none were salvaged, though understandable that the small and over-worked staff of the game department did not undertake the task – here was a glaring example of the need for more biologists in the field in Africa."

He also during this trip started work on using tranquiliser drugs and a projectile syringe gun to immobilise and capture large mammals and he wrote about this in a report for the Wellcome Institute.

After visiting Kenya and northern Rhodesia he was extremely excited about the scope for work with the game animals "and how great the potential is for the study of almost any aspect of the life of these mammals and of almost every species".

He wrote that the study of the behaviour of species threatened with extinction "should have the highest priority" and that the species that need to be studied with the "utmost urgency" were the elephants, the rhinoceros and the buffalo, which were causing immense habitat destruction. "The prospect of having to slaughter thousands of elephants in the next few years is an imminent one," he pointed out.

He advised on the need for an office "that will collate information about game research in Africa and pass on information about the game-cropping schemes and other projects – it is clear that zoologists themselves have an active part to play in such developments". This was the point where Peter realised that Africa was where he wanted to be.

A magnificent elephant in the Serengeti, photographed by Peter

# Pottery, the Natural History Museum and archaeozoology: Juliet's early career

# 7

J uliet's first introduction to archaeology was at the age of nine when she and her cousin Tristan found stone and bits of pottery when they were on a kopje (rocky hill) in Rhodesia, and took the pottery to the museum in the capital, Salisbury. She carried on being fascinated with ancient artefacts but at boarding school was told that she couldn't read archaeology at university because she hadn't studied classical Greek. Instead she was encouraged to think about being a medic and in 1951 started her degree at the Old Royal Free Hospital in Gray's Inn Road, central London. She described it as "a dismal place" and soon gave it up to go and work in a small art gallery where she learned "the rudiments of cleaning pictures".

When there, she heard about a new course in archaeological technique at the Institute of Archaeology, at St John's Lodge in Regent's Park, she was "bewitched by the building, the people in it, the park and the nearness of the Zoo, and I gleefully signed up to do the course for the year 1953-54". There were about 20 students and they learnt how to "reconstruct pots with glue, plasticine and plaster of Paris and how to clean coins and coat them with the new preservative of polyvinyl."

She was still undecided, however, about what to do with her life and on 4 June 1953, wrote to her cousin Irene Whitmore-Jones, who lived at Chastleton, about going to stay with her and the Queen's coronation.

> *Dear Cousin Irene, I am afraid as usual I must repeat my most humble apologies for not writing before. The coronation and leaving the family in London for the last week has pretty well filled every minute of the day and I have not done those things I ought to have done. I talked to Papa about leaving the job etc and also to my employers who are very loath for me to leave until the end of July and as I originally said I would stay until October I think I'd better stay until then. Then if you have no one in August and September to stay with you I could come then. I may have to start working like a slave at Latin to go to the Courtauld Institute to do a degree in History of Art but this is rather vague. I do wish I could think of something really sensible and plausible to do which is the crux of the matter at the moment. I do hope you are well and enjoyed the coronation festivities. We all had a wonderful view in perfect comfort and luxury from the National Gallery. The procession really could not have been more splendid or impressive.*
> *Yours very sincerely Juliet"*

While working on the artefacts at the Institute of Archaeology she also went to course lectures given by the great archaeologists of the day – Gordon Childe, Mortimer Wheeler, Max Mallowan, Kathleen Kenyon and Frederick Zeuner. Juliet said she had many "good, bad and amusing" memories of her year at the institute. One bad moment was when her teacher Miss Gedye was showing some people around the cases of restored pots and she lifted the sloping glass lid of a case, took the re-

constructed pot out, but failed to put it far enough back in. Trying to be helpful, Juliet held the lid open and then put it down, crushing the pot into fragments, and ended up having to glue it back together again.

Juliet was especially interested in restoring animal skulls – and this was to spark her fascination with animal remains from archaeological sites. Archaeology in the 1950s was just emerging from being a romantic occupation mainly pursued by dedicated amateurs who often used their own private incomes to fund their excavations, and whose main aim was the retrieval of antiquities. As Juliet later described, "the study of palaeontology and human evolution was acceptable as research, but in most archaeological excavations, the animal remains that filled the trenches were considered to be a troublesome by-product of the antiquities or structural remains and all but the most complete were usually reburied with the soil".

The first skull she restored was that of a hyaena from Dr Antony Sutcliffe's cave excavations in Devon. It was through this work that Juliet had her first personal contact with Professor Frederick Everard Zeuner, the great German paleontologist and archaeologist who had recently set up a department of environmental archaeology. Juliet described him as "one of the last of the great self-taught polymaths in the natural sciences who had been trained in the pre-war German school of strict attention to detail in all undertakings". Under Zeuner's guidance, archaeozoology was being established as a new discipline involving the identification of often fragmentary bones and teeth, which requires not only a wide knowledge of comparative osteology, but also an appreciation of the significance of these remains to the history of the people who accumulated them.

Sutcliffe, who had just finished his PhD under Zeuner, "became a lifelong colleague and friend". The next skull she restored was one of the plaster decorated skulls from Jericho, which had just been excavated. During the summer term at the institute, Zeuner led several day trips to see archaeological and geological sites around the south of England. It was at one of these trips, that Juliet met Peter, "my future husband, a physiologist interested in archaeology".

At one interview with Professor Zeuner he told Juliet that she was "wasting her time" and that she should go and get a degree in zoology and then come back and work with him. He arranged for her to enroll at the Chelsea College, University of London to do a three-year degree course in zoology and geology, which she duly began in the autumn term of 1954, but she kept "close contacts with archaeology and the institute".

In the summer of 1954 Juliet went to Greece as a volunteer to work on the Bronze Age excavation of Emporio on Chios under Sinclair Hood, who was the director of the British School of Archaeology at Athens. It was a "marvellous experience" and she met many interesting people including Michael Ventris, the architect and cryptographer, and his wife Betty, who became lifelong friends, and also John Boardman, and Richard Garnet, who, on a boat in the bay, was pioneering underwater archaeology.

In 1955 she went to Knossos, on Crete, to restore the human skulls from Sinclair's excavation for the anthropologists Jack Trevor and

In Orkney, 1956 excavation with Gordon Childe

Bernard Campbell, staying in the Villa Ariadne. In 1956 she went on a summer school in Orkney and Shetland, led by the eminent archaeologist Vere Gordon Childe, the year before his death, and in 1957, she went on the excavation of Bronze Age Snail Down in Wiltshire that was directed by Nick Thomas and Charles Thomas. While she was there she got the results of her degree – a first, which enabled her to begin work on a PhD with Zeuner in the autumn term.

Juliet felt very lucky to be working under Zeuner's guidance. His research had been on integrating British and Continental studies on the dating of the Quaternary, but he had also become interested in mammalian remains and in animal domestication and in establishing the new discipline of archaeozoology. As Juliet described: "I had little choice in what I was to study. I was to take over the animal remains from three sites that were in the Institute waiting to be worked on, and Zeuner arranged for me and the collections to be moved to the Osteology Room at the Natural History Museum, where I spent the next four years trying to get some sort of scientific link out of the material from the widely different sites." This first introduction to the Natural History Museum led to her lifelong work there and her role in establishing archaeozoology as a recognised scientific subject.

Zeuner became a family friend and went to meals with Peter and Juliet in their "tiny house" at 36 Southwood Lane in Highgate. Juliet recalled how "on one occasion there was nowhere for him to sit because our first baby was asleep on the only armchair and couldn't be awakened because she would have screamed". Zeuner oversaw her research and in 1966 she was awarded her PhD on mammalian faunas from prehistoric sites in India and western Asia and on faunal remains from excavations at Jericho Tell in Palestine.

Juliet on a boat trip in Greece, 1954

# Civil war, a mini zoo
# and ecology: Biafra 1966

# 8

P eter and Juliet had become pioneers in a new movement that was starting up in the 1960s – to understand animal behaviour in the wild with as little human interference as possible. Where previously animals were hunted, shot and stuffed, now they were being observed from a discreet distance in their natural habitat – with young biologists in Africa leading the way. George Schaller began studying the mountain gorillas in the Virunga Volcanoes in 1959, followed by Diane Fossey and Louis Leakey, and in 1960 Jane Goodall began her famous study of chimpanzees in the Gombe Stream Reserve in Tanganyika. Thomas Struhsaker studied the Red Colobus monkeys in Cameroon and Ian Douglas-Hamilton began studying elephants in Kenya in 1965. Studies of wild large mammals began in the Serengeti Park in 1961 and the Nuffield Unit of Tropical Animal Ecology got going in the Queen Elizabeth National Park in Uganda in the same year. Ecology was developing as the scientific study of how organisms interact with each other and their environment, and Peter and Juliet jumped at the chance to be part of this.

On 28 June 1966 Peter received a letter from Professor Michael

Abercromie of University College London offering him the post of senior lecturer in the Department of Zoology and Comparative Anatomy at UCL for a period of five years from 1 July 1966 to 30 June 1971, with "at the outset a period of not less than two years at the University of Nigeria, Nsukka". There he was to be "head of the newly constituted Biological Sciences Group, with the rank and title of Professor". It was a really exciting appointment that was arranged between UCL, the University of Nsukka and the Ministry of Overseas Development.

The letter of appointment stated: "During that period you will receive salary at the rate of £3,000 per annum (the standard professorial rate at Nsukka) plus 20% supplements provided by the Ministry of Overseas Development, ie a total of £3,600 per annum; together with the usual allowances payable to academic staff of the university, and provision of residential accommodation. The duties at Nsukka will be to take general responsibility for organising and developing the teaching of both undergraduate and postgraduate students in the Biological Sciences Group, to take an appropriate share in that teaching, and to do all in your power, by research and otherwise, to promote the advancement of your subject. It is assumed at the moment that you will be leaving for Nigeria on 15 August." It was a hugely inspiring and challenging opportunity for both Peter and Juliet.

But it was also an extraordinary move to make against the backdrop of civil war and political instability in Nigeria. A military coup in January 1966 had led to the downfall of the civilian government that had ruled Nigeria since independence in 1960. Soldiers, led by Kaduna Nzeogwu and Emmanuel Ifeajuna, killed 22 people including the prime minister of Nigeria, many senior politicians and senior Army officers. Johnson Aguiyi-Ironsi, the commander of the army, took power – he was an Igbo, the most numerous and powerful ethnic group in south-eastern Nigeria. After four months, Ironsi announced a new constitution and abolished Nigeria's semi-autonomous regions. Fearing political domination by the Igbos, the northern Nigerians launched a series of pogroms in northern cities and from June through to October 1966, the pogroms killed an estimated 80,000 to 100,000 Igbo, half of them children, and caused a million to two million people to flee to the Eastern Region. In July, Ironsi was deposed in a northern-led coup. The new government, led by Yakubu Gowon, restored the regional system but was opposed by the Igbos.

It was in the midst of this conflict and violence that the British government told Peter that it believed major turmoil in Nigeria was unlikely, "and so we continued planning for our project" wrote 21-year-old John

John camping in the rainforest

Oates, a biologist studying lorisid primates, who took a two-year appointment as Peter's research assistant and accompanied him to Nsukka to begin work on his PhD. John wrote in his book, *Myth and Reality in the Rainforest: how conservation strategies are failing*, that the idea of going to live in Nigeria "seemed a very attractive option, because Peter Jewell was not only a leading mammalian ecologist, he also had strong commitment to conservation, a subject that increasingly interested me".

And so on 15 August 1966, the family set off for Nigeria – their house in Highgate was rented out and all their possessions put into storage. As Juliet wrote: "Peter took all of his work to Nigeria and a huge number of index punch cards – we flew to Nsukka with no house arranged and rented a bungalow". She described the first three months as "very difficult" because she had "nothing to do", by which she meant that she had no academic work. Day to day she was busy sorting out a school for us girls, organising the house and looking after the growing number of animals that arrived at the zoology department.

During their time in Nigeria, both Peter and Juliet wrote regularly to their best friends, Alan and Christian Ness, and Juliet also wrote regularly to her aunt Doreen (the sister of her mother and aunt Kathleen). These letters are an extraordinary record of their daily life and the escalation of the Biafran war.

On 6 September 1966 Juliet wrote her first letter to Alan and Christian, which describes how unsettled they were feeling:

> Dearest Alan and Christian,
> I fear we are not finding it easy to settle in here. It is wet and muggy and apparently hardly ever sunny. For in the rainy season, as now, it rains all the time and in the dry season the cold harmattan winds blow sand over the country from the Sahara and there is a continual heavy haze. It is not hot now. In fact we are often cold. The campus is a vast rambling assemblage of buildings surrounded by a tight circle of African villages.
>
> There are about 3,000 students and I suppose 2,000 staff and others. Twelve of these are British, rather more American and a few Dutch. The political situation here is bad and it is not safe to travel out of eastern Nigeria, mainly because once out it is very difficult to get back in. If Peter wants to go to the Cameroons, further East, he has to go West 300 miles to Lagos to get a re-entry permit first! So this looks as though it has put paid to any faint hopes he had

of doing any worthwhile fieldwork. If the East secedes, which it wishes to do, I expect we would be returned to London so we feel insecure.

We have bought an ancient Land Rover because P doesn't want to invest too much money here with things as they are. Now he fears it may be older than we thought and we may lose money on it – the engine has the most sinister whine to it. On my part my feet feel black and blue from driving it but I must admit to feeling spiritually one up on all the other university wives when they see me swooping about in it. Campus life is based on the American pattern and dreary in the extreme. I am hoping to do some work in the one-man archaeology department. This is of course paradise for entomologists – the butterflies and birds are stunning but all the mammals have been eaten hundreds, if not thousands, of years ago. I haven't seen a single wild mammal. The children seem very content to spend their days tending their caterpillars.
Much love, Juliet

On 17 September 1966 Juliet wrote her first letter to her aunt, describing how they were settling in:

"At first I didn't have nearly enough to do each day and I felt very low as a result! But we are getting used to everything now. All shopping is done in markets and these markets are a way of life for the people. Yesterday we went to Onitsha which has the biggest market in West Africa. It was incredibly noisy and crowded and we felt very lost but we bought some lovely indigo blue West African cloth for curtains. We are due to move into our house next week *if the painters have finished cleaning it up and our trunks should also arrive soon. So far we have been almost camping in a huge empty house that makes us feel as though we are living in a public swimming bath.*

*The children all start school tomorrow although I don't know whether Rebecca will agree to stay at the nursery school without me. I have to get curtains made and school uniforms. Daily life seems to require even more organisation than in London! We don't want to spend a penny more than we have to in case we have to leave in a hurry. The political situation shows no sign of easing and everyone is feeling very unsettled about the future.*

*All our love, Juliet.*

Topsy and Sarah holding Dragon and Greeney, their chameleons

John Oates arrived in Nsukka on 8 September 1966, and the political situation was already worsening – he wrote in his book that they found "newly installed military checkpoints on the road between Enugu airport and Nsukka, and soon after my arrival a new and more terrible wave of massacres began in the north, in which tens of thousands of Igbos are thought to have died."

On 1 November 1966 Juliet wrote to her aunt:

My dearest Aunt,

Thank you so much for your letter received today. One of the many peculiarities of this post is that letters from you [Doreen lived in Wiltshire] seem to arrive quicker than from London. We have been travelling about a little more lately which is hot and exhausting and extremely irritating when we are held up in road blocks lasting an hour or more waiting to have the car searched by policemen.

We went on a very exciting journey North into the Northern Region and stayed a weekend with a fabulous missionary family who lived in a real old style homestead and we had pancakes and wild honey for breakfast. P had to collect some duikers from them to bring back for the little zoo here so we all went for the trip. But we had to take enough petrol for our two landrovers to get there and back, because all services have broken down and there is no petrol for sale (outside the Black Market) in the North. This weekend we are going to stay on a cattle ranch on the borders of the Cameroon mountains. We are looking forward to this very much because it is real mountains and the climate is cool and you can get fresh milk and butter.

We have recently bought a transistor radio on which we can actually get the BBC in London so we are not feeling quite so isolated. Yes, we did hear about Aberfan [the Welsh coal mining disaster where a colliery tip collapsed into homes and a school, killing 116 children and 28 adults] and felt quite numbed about it. Since we got here we seem to have been constantly surrounded by death. We have been told by a friend that the hospital in Enugu looks like the 1914-18 war. There are wounded refu-

*gees from the North everywhere and it really seems a mad world.*
*I don't think I would have come with the children if we had had*
*any idea how bad the situation would be here.*
*All our love, Juliet*

As well as trying to establish their work and home life, Peter and Juliet also became the guardians of a mini zoo on the university campus as people kept giving them their stray and sick animals, and some of these animals became family pets. They cared for a huge python that was brought to the zoology department in a box cage and was permanently curled up until Peter had a bigger cage made for it in the university and watched it unfurl. They were also given dik-dik – little antelope – and their most fiercesome pet, Juma, the baby chimpanzee. She was given to Juliet by some colleagues who were leaving the country. She lived on the veranda and slept in the garage and Juliet always said in later life that she felt terribly guilty about owning her.

Peter and John's research centred on studying the nocturnal tree-dwelling, small mammals, pottos (Perodicticus potto) and angwantibos (Arctocebus calabarensis). In their book *Ecological Observations on the Lorisoid Primates of African Lowland Forest* they wrote: "The

two species of potto are the only captive lorisoids we have studied. Most of them were brought by hunters and farmers to the University Zoo at Nsukka, and several different types of study have been carried out. In small box cages food-preference tests were

Juma and Topsy on the verandah

Peter with three angwantibos

made and growth rates were measured. In a large outdoor cage, in the Biological Garden at Nsukka, interactions between individual angwantibos were investigated, and similar work was started on the potto."

John also describes how at night they observed the angwantibos by torchlight or by a simple lighting system installed on the cage. "Collars were devised to enable the identification of individual animals. The collars were made of Dayglo plastic, with inset reflective plastic squares. They were attached to several animals and proved effective and long-lasting, and similar collars were developed with a view to their use on wild animals."

In his article, *The Wildlife of Biafra*, in the journal Animals – vol 11 no 6, John wrote: "A fascinating way of investigating the mammal population was to walk through the reserve (which is only two square miles and covered in planted trees) beside the town of Onitsha on the banks of the Niger at night with a head torch. At night you can locate animals by the reflections from their eyes. Angwantibos were very commonly seen climbing stealthily through the branches of the planted trees. Many zoologists have considered angwantibos to be extremely rare animals, but in fact they are one of the few species to have successfully exploited

John in the rainforest

the "destroyed" habitat produced by man."

John became acutely aware of "just how threatened some African rain forests and their wildlife were becoming" – large areas of land were given to Igbo refugees for farming, and the hunting of animals for food was intense, "this hunting was largely uncontrolled because management was directed toward tree crops rather than the ecosystem as a whole; indeed, forest officers themselves were often serious hunters".

Peter and John started making the case for the protection of Eastern Nigerian forests and their neglected wildlife, arguing that "there should be more emphasis on the conservation of the whole biological community than on the management of trees for commercial exploitation". But they were voices, said John, "literally crying in the wilderness, for the political tensions had been increasing through our stay at Nsukka and conservation was low on the agenda".

On 8 November 1966 Juliet wrote to her aunt describing an exploratory trip the family took to Obudu in the Cameroons to find out more about the wildlife.

My Dearest Aunt,
Last Thursday we went to stay for 4 days at Obudu. This is a cattle ranch on the borders of the Cameroon mountains and once we

got there we enjoyed it very much. We all went riding and swimming in an icy mountain river and Peter spent one whole day trekking round the forest reserves on horseback with guides.

We went because Peter wanted to find out what sort of animal life there is in these forests. The answer is practically none, which is disheartening as we were all hoping it would be a good place for fieldwork. The ranch is 250 miles from here and is an easy drive except for the last 9 miles when you have to climb 3,000 feet. We had gone up about 3 miles of this when the landrover didn't make a hair-pin bend. So Peter tried to reverse, whereupon the gear lever snapped off and came away in his hands!

Fortunately the car was locked in second gear and we crept up the rest of the way in this gear and 4-wheel drive! They fixed on a new gear level at the ranch but on the way back some washers went which meant that air kept getting into the clutch and break system. So every half hour we had to stop and "bleed" the clutch and let the air out. And of course every time we stopped at the police blocks the car wouldn't start again and we had to ask the policemen to push us. This happened six times on the way back. They stop you at a road block and you wait in a queue of cars (sometimes for an hour) and then about 3 policemen and maybe 2 soldiers all search you and all your possessions. But we all enjoyed the break from Nsukka – it was really lovely in the mountains – lush rainforest with tree ferns and marvellous views. We went out late one night with torches and looked for bush babies and other night-living creatures. We saw quite a lot and it was great fun.

We shall stay here now until the Christmas holidays. We want to try and drive down to Calabar then which I am sure is an interesting place but it will be fearfully hot. The children are all well on the whole but they are becoming most lethargic – maybe this is not a bad thing! I will write again soon.

Very much love, Juliet

On 14 November Juliet wrote again to her aunt:

My dearest Aunt, the parcel of ribbons, sponges and cologne arrived on Saturday intact and I only had to pay 3 shillings customs, Thank you so very much. Now I feel really luxurious in the bath, if at no other time!

I have made hair bands for the children and they already look much tidier and less like Yorkshire terriers. We have also had 3 copies of The Field already and have enjoyed reading it enormously; Peter says we must pass the copies on to the university library when we have finished with them so they will certainly get a lot of reading. We are buying bicycles for the children, at vast cost, because it will be so much easier for them to learn to ride here than on the suicidal English roads.

Sarah and Topsy are the only English children in the University school, the others being about 120 Nigerians, 20 Americans and 5 Indians. Topsy is getting on fine but Sarah is rather scared of the rigid discipline and I think the Nigerian girls tease her a bit. She is too sensitive and cries easily but what can one do about it? She can read quite fluently now.

*Peter is snowed under with administrative work, but seems to remain remarkably calm. All my love Juliet*

And on Sunday, 27 Nov 1966, Juliet wrote to the Nesses:

Sarah and Topsy at school

*Dearest Nesses, it seems like a perpetual August here. I cannot believe it is November. The only thing to tell one that time passes is that hair grows longer and clothes wear out at fantastic rate. There is a perennial water shortage here because they cannot keep the borehole machinery working. The tragedy about this episode in our lives is not only was it one of those utterly predictable but unavoidable mistakes that people with P's and my temperaments make at sometime during one's life but also the whole conception of the job was a mistake. The zoology and botany department at Nsukka do not want to be coordinated into a Department of biological science, least of all by an Englishman ... so you can imagine what this makes Peter feel like. Now because of the crisis a crash programme has been put on to start a medical school. Of course P has been landed on to be chief organiser, this means committee meetings ad infinitum (sometimes he gets home at 1:30 AM). Another worry is that he cannot find a doctor who will prescribe more than four sleeping tablets at a time.*

*I am actually very busy by a stroke of luck the archaeology depart-*

Sarah wearing her White Horse Whisky necklace – Peter and Juliet loved to drink!

ment has recently set up a museum in a building that had been built as a super laundry. Well there has never been water for a laundry and machinery still sits there. It is the only building on the campus which has room to spare. So I have a very grand desk there and everything I could wish for, for work. I have a much better place, in fact, than Peter.

So I go and busy myself there every morning and write up my work on the Jericho bones. I am also doing some demonstrating in zoology practicals. This is a crazy setup – I am looking at tapeworms with my class of 90 students but there are only a few petrie dishes, a few chairs, some microscopes, some pickled specimens but no water and no slides. Juma, the chimp, has heavy infestations of tapeworm and round worm – so I have worms at home as well at work there. So far the family, to our knowledge, have only caught roundworms and we are all having to drink vast quantities of the most loathesome ever medicine.

Much love to you all Juliet

On 8 December Peter wrote to Alan Ness:

My dear Alan, my thanks for your long letter. Quite clogged up now with petty admin. Our pets at home now comprise: 1 Chimpanzee, 1 Angwantibo, 1 Ground squirrel, 3 chameleons, 1 tortoise.

Peter and Juma

*Many insects and other lower orders also have adopted us, including thread worms who now infect the whole family including the chimpanzee! Love and greetings P*

On 13 December Juliet wrote to her colleagues at the Natural History Museum:

*Dear Judith and Dr Fraser,*
*It is hard to believe it is December. The climate does go from wet to dry, but with little change of temperature. We have got through the wet season and are now in the dry which lasts till March or so. The last few days have seen the beginning of the Harmattan – the*

hot winds from the Sahara that envelop everything in sandy dust. It is most weird, the landscape has closed in so that one can barely see a quarter of a mile in any one direction and spectacles are continually covered with a fine film of dust. Sad to get away from smoke fumes only to end up in dust storms!

Life here is very weird – we managed to arrive during about the worst month Nigeria has ever seen from the political point of view and for weeks we were expecting to be evacuated at any moment. There really have been the most terrible massacres in the North and now the small Eastern Region is overrun by more than a million refugees. This of course has made a tremendous difference to life in the university. Now it is so overcrowded with refugee students and staff that nobody seems to know what he is meant to be doing. Peter is having a great struggle to keep everybody's head above water in his department and, needless to say, he has not been able to start any serious field work.

I can't say that we are enjoying life at Nsukka but I suppose you could say we are "settled down!". There are no large mammals to be seen but Peter has found that lorisoids are amazingly common. If he can find some way to trap them they could be a very interesting group of animals to study. With best wishes to you both for Christmas and the New Year, Yours Juliet.

Letterheads designed by Peter and Juliet for
their airmail writing paper

# Field trips, hazy days and evacuation: Biafra 1967

# 9

On 23 December 1966 Peter wrote to Alan from Victoria, Cameroon:

*Two days after the winter solstice and tomorrow Christmas Eve. I have wanted to write sooner but have had little heart for it. We have come to the Cameroons for a week and are staying at Victoria in a small hotel overlooking the sea. First term is over and I am pretty disheartened. I don't think I am being or can be effective. JUAC (Joint Universities Advisory Committee) is supposed to help the development of the University of Nigeria.*

*Michigan State has about 30 people seconded here. On the staff are professors, lecturers, administrators and advisors. London has three, one in law, one in French and me. What is the point? I have no backing worth speaking of, nothing to offer to help support research, the Americans put up big installations for the Agriculture department and it flourishes. Biological sciences remain the Cinderella without a fairy godmother. It is hopelessly demoralising to try to do everything on one's own. I spent hours and days trying to get*

Driving to Victoria, Cameroon

a few microscopes for biology. It is unbelievably hopeless really. Well-intentioned, I suppose, on the part of London University but completely ineffective in execution. We did climb a few 1000 feet up Mt Cameroon but only passed though secondary forest with many clearings for cultivation and fired patches. Interestingly a great many small birds in both species and numbers. Many dark in colour. P

On Saturday, 7 January 1967, Juliet wrote to her aunt:

My dearest Aunt, We got back from Victoria last Saturday, uneventfully. The roads didn't seem nearly so fearsome as when we first drove over them and the police blocks were unusually friendly. We assumed because it was New Year's Eve. We all feel much better for the holiday and ready for struggling with our second term which has just started.

Peter has gone off for the weekend to Port Harcourt with 40 students on a field trip. I now have a friend in the form of a policeman from the local prison who bicycles down twice a week to sell me vast quantities of bananas and fresh vegetables from the prison garden. At present we are flooded with Cape gooseberries and I am busy making jam.

The weather is not very pleasant here now, it is hot and very dry and the Harmattan winds are blowing sand from the Sahara everywhere so there is a heavy haze all over the country and thick dust everywhere. One feels quite gummed up with it. But at last the swimming pool is open and we go there most afternoons. Topsy really swims very well now. And Sarah is getting on well with riding her bicycle although she finds it difficult to stop which has led to some very nasty moments! We are getting much more used to life in Nigeria now. The thing is one has to learn to live at so much slower rate than in London! At first I was in a perpetual state of irritation at having to wait hours to get anything done. Now I travel everywhere with a book and read while waiting. I do hope that you are feeling well now and that you have a very good 1967. All my love Juliet

Christmas 1966 at the Miramare Hotel, Victoria (now Limbe), Cameroon

On 13 January 1967 Peter wrote to Alan again:

*Today and yesterday are public holidays. Hoorah! But when was it announced that they would be recognised here? Just the day before! I had to cancel several committee meetings I had arranged and practical classes. Now all will have to be arranged again. Nothing is done at the first request here no matter how urgent it is. I have no desk, no proper room, no budget, but I have got a set of rubber stamps! I have made myself a police pass with a passport photo and my stamps work marvels at police roadblocks.*

*Have just heard that the university will not pay for me to attend a Food and Agriculture Organisation (FAO) wildlife meeting in Fort Lamy Chad. What is the point of being in West Africa and not taking part. How to get visas to go to Republique Centre Africaine or is it Chad? This means a journey to Lagos in the west through innumerable police blocks. Frustration is the permanent state of affairs here it doesn't matter what one tries to push through the administration nothing ever happens. So I have to waste hours of time chasing things up it is absolutely maddening. It has been good to pass Christmas with no fuss, no presents, no nonsense just a short holiday by the tropical sea in the Cameroons. Much better. P*

On Tuesday. 22 January 1967 Juliet wrote to her aunt:

*My dearest Aunt, thank you very much for your letter of the 7th. I am sorry I haven't written sooner. I usually write letters after lunch and it is so hot now – I haven't the energy! I hope by now you will have had at least one letter from me since we got back to Nsukka.*

*Everyone is well although hot. We have a glut of tomatoes in the garden and have to eat vast quantities at every meal.*

*The house is so full of crates with animals in them that when someone came to call the other day his first words were "goodness are you leaving!" He thought we were packing up – I wish we were. I spend much time brooding on where the children will be able to go to school when we get back to London.*

*Peter goes away for two weeks next week. He is going to an exciting meeting (wild life etc) at Fort Lame in Chad – on the edge of the Sahara. I hope he doesn't get roasted. It is said to be the most expensive capital in the world because it is so far from the sea and everything has to be flown there.*

*The children seem very content with their daily routine – school in the mornings, rest after lunch, then swimming, then tea, then bed! I expect it is good for them. They are joining in better with the neighbouring Nigerian children now which is very nice – they catch grasshoppers together for all our animals.*
*Very much love, Juliet*

On 1 February 1967 Peter wrote to Alan describing his increasing unhappiness and frustration with his job:

*My dear Alan,*
*2 years = 24 months, 3 months leave = 21 months; Aug-Jan = 5 months gone. Months still to go = 16. That is how we reckon time here. Many thanks for your long letter. Life goes on but who wants*

to waste 2 yrs, sorry 16 months, when he is already 41? Air still dust laden from the Harmattan. The American vet here accidentally killed his wife by overdosing her with antimalarial tabs – calculated it on the basis for a cow. Exactly what you'd expect. Fondest greetings. Peter

On 25 February Juliet wrote to her aunt:

My Dearest Aunt, thank you so much for your two-volume letter of February 18th that arrived yesterday. Yes, I am afraid several of your letters and mine must have gone astray – an awful lot of ours have failed to reach England lately. We have had a terribly hectic week with grand parties every night. A joint University Advisory Committee (professors from England and America) have been here to inspect the university and we have been involved in so much entertaining and discussion that I haven't known whether I am on my head or my heels. But they are mostly gone now and I fear life will seem doubly quiet without them. Although it is so hot now it is quite a relief. I feel as though I were ten months pregnant and drag myself around from chore to chore on leaden legs – just because it is so hot and fantastically humid.

The grandest party we went to last week was given by the Military Governor at the State House Enugu for the visiting professors. We drove up to the closed gates in our old Land Rover and all togged up in our best clothes (me in stockings for the first time since we got here). Where upon Peter and the car were completely gone over and through in a detailed search by about 6 policemen. We were then allowed to drive in and left the car.

*The Military Governor was followed everywhere by soldiers who were so heavily armed that they could hardly walk! Nigeria as a whole and the East in particu-*

Celebrating Biafra Day – 30 May 1967

*lar is not an easy place to live in. The country has become a real police state and carries all the problems that this brings in its wake. The police checks are getting worse and several British men have been seriously beaten up by the soldiers for no reason other than that they are British.*

*The house is fuller than ever of baby animals that are fostered on to me by the small zoo here. So I am back to heating up bottles of milk every few hours – very trying and not at all satisfying!*
*I have been working very hard in the Archaeology Department but will have to take the next week off because our baby nurse has had to suddenly go home – her brother's child has died. Children die here at a horrifying rate and it is really terrible to experience it happen at first hand. I do hope you will get this letter at least.*
*All my love Juliet.*

The political situation was rapidly worsening: as John wrote in his book *Myth and Reality in the Rainforest: how conservation strategies are fail-*

*ing*: "On May 30 1967 Lieutenant Colonel Odumegwu Ojukwu declared that Eastern Nigeria was seceding from the federation as the independent nation of Biafra." Civil war broke out between Nigeria and Biafra in July 1967 and as John wrote: "In the tense atmosphere that followed, in which the Biafran people were constantly warned of the dangers from traitors and saboteurs, travel and fieldwork became very difficult. Expatriates at the university began to hold meetings to discuss what they should do in the event of war; clear differences soon emerged between the professional, well-organised American plans and the amateurish plans of the British."

In June 1967 the political situation became so dangerous that it was decided Peter and Juliet and the family had to evacuate. As Juliet wrote later:

> "We were meant to be in Nigeria for three to five years but in the summer of 1967 the Biafran war came to a head and we wondered what to do. One night we were told to go to Port Harcourt – we all gathered in a church hall with American and English families. I went to the loo with a woman and she said her child was dying – I slapped the child on its back – it had choked and survived. We went from Port Harcourt to Lagos. Then to Johannesburg then to Harare. The children wore red shorts and t-shirts and got chewing gum. I had no contact with Peter or John Oates – they walked to the river Niger and got in a boat carrying their briefcases."

John described his departure in his book:

> "In early June, most dependents of expatriates were evacuated and on July 1, as BBC broadcast predicted imminent war, most remaining expatriates left Nsukka. I followed two days later, taking a small boat across the Niger from Onitsha, with most of my research notes

*and a few personal belongings crammed into the single suitcase I
was allowed to carry. On July 7 Nigerian federal forces invaded Biafra, with one of their first attacks directed against Nsukka. The grue-
some war dragged on until January 1970."*

Peter joined Juliet and the children at her aunt Kathleen's house in Harare.
Peter arranged a long trip to England – via Kenya, Uganda, Rome – which
Juliet described: "It was lovely driving along the roads in Uganda – we
all enjoyed that. We flew in small planes but I got Meniere's syndrome
and became very ill as I temporarily lost the balance in my ears. We
lost all our work, research notes our books and all the punch cards with
Peter's work – 2,000 of them."

The animals were all left behind and Juma tied in a cage. After the war
ended, Anita Mackie, a great friend of Peter and Juliet's, went back to

Last picture of Juma, found in the
house after the war ended

the house – it was completely ransacked
and empty and the only things she found
were two photographs of Juma.

Years later Juliet wrote to John
Oates saying:

*"Taking on Juma and thinking we
could look after her was completely
naïve on my part. We thought we were
doing a good deed but it was selfish
and cruel and it is perhaps the decision I most regret taking during my life,
although we could not have envisaged
the final act of having to leave her in a*

small cage with the Biafran war raging around the campus, probably to have been eaten by starving people. What of course we
should have done when asked to take her on after our arrival at
the University of Nsukka was to have searched for a rescue centre where she could have been with other chimps, but in those days
this would have been very difficult to organize, and we were new
to the country."

John replied:

"I'm saddened that you feel so bad about Juma. I can understand
why, on reflection, you feel as you do, and that shows what a
good person you are. But when you took on Juma you were a different person (inevitably more naive) living in a different world.
Although there were political tensions, there was little real expec-
tation of a terrible civil war in those early months at Nsukka.
Keeping Juma surely seemed the right thing to do for her, and
something that would provide fascination for your daughters. I can
see how in retrospect you'd wish you'd found a rescue centre, but
ape rescue centres didn't exist then in Africa as far as I know, and
the zoos in Nigeria were all pretty ropey. Terrible things happened
to people in Nigeria during the civil war; I think you should con-
sider Juma as perhaps another unfortunate casualty of war. In any
case, you don't know that she was eaten; Nsukka was occupied
quite early on in the conflict by the federal army, after little fighting, so she might initially have become a soldier's pet."

Once they were all in Rhodesia, Peter wrote from Salisbury to Alan on
20 July 1967:

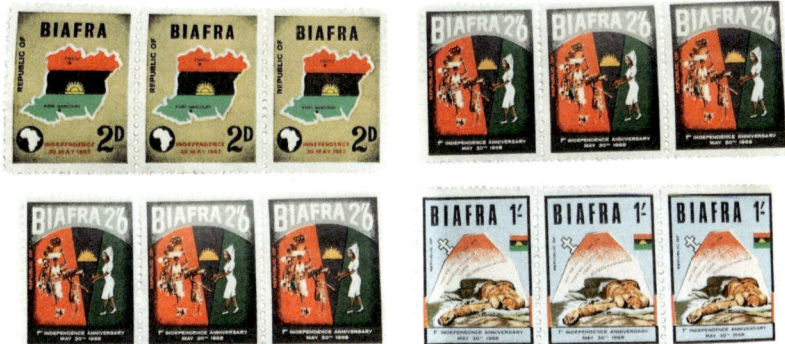

Biafran stamps

*Dear Alan, I had many days of quiet thinking by myself at Nsukka – there were sad faces when I had to leave but my last days were uneventful – if I had not been going to the symposium in South Africa I would still have been there when the northern bandits attacked. Many Brits, however, failed to keep a stiff upper lip and would not wait for me on July 1st and went off to the river Niger before our agreed departure time. So I had to get two new-found friends – not averse to a whisky and ice to pass the last hours of the day – to drive me to the river in my own Land Rover. Farewell. They drove it back but where is it now?*

*That night I stayed with Christians and having taken of the hospitality usually offered to God-fearing travellers I crossed the Niger next day in a large canoe and eventually got to Benin. No time to look at the bronzes. On to Lagos, the lair of the imperialist puppet, leader of feudal junta and bloodstained bandit. Tool of Britain. The Dictator Gowon.*

*Red black and green. Colours of the brave Biafra flag. Red for the blood of the slaughtered, black for mourning, green for the new tomorrow. Will it come? On the black a rising sun. Golden. Goodbye Biafra.*

*As our leader Colonel Ojukwu said "no power in Black Africa can suppress Biafra". Biafra claims to have retaken lost ground including Nsukka. What ho. Is the Jewells' house in flames. Are the labs demolished. Where are Juliet's punch cards of the animal remains from Jericho? Two years of hard work. Where are Prof Jewell's filing cards, reprint collection, and colour transparencies collected over 10 years? Burning well. I would like to be there to see them burn but few are privileged to attend their own funeral. The link between University College London and the University of Nigeria. I didn't realise that only one link in the chain would be exposed for breaking. Self. Some people worry that they will leave Nigeria with bilharzia and hookworm. Have they ever thought of leaving with nothing? We shall remember 1967.*
*Love Peter*

On 11 January 1970 Nigerian forces captured Owerri, one of the last Biafran strongholds, and Colonel Ojukwu was forced to flee to the Ivory Coast. Four days later Biafra surrendered to Nigeria.

UNIVERSITY OF ~~NIGERIA~~ BIAFRA

STAFF IDENTIFICATION CARD

The Validity of this Card

Expires on   30th June, 1968.

SIGNATURE OF BEARER

THIS IS TO CERTIFY THAT

Prof. P. A. Jewell

whose photograph and signature appear on the
opposite page is employed by the
University of Nigeria as

Director, Division of Biological Sciences

Date of Issue   1st July, 1967.

Validity Expires   30th June, 1968.

REGISTRAR

# Old bones, skeletons and dogs: Juliet's career takes off

# 10

eter and Juliet and their girls left Orange Grove on 16 August 1967 and flew to Johannesburg, then on to Entebbe, Nairobi, Rome, and finally London, arriving on 24 August. By the end of the year the family were back to their house in Jackson's Lane, Highgate.

After settling back in London, Juliet resumed working part-time at the Natural History Museum and in 1969 she was offered a post as full-time senior research worker in the mammal section – cataloguing the collection of animal bones that archaeologists had been sending back for nearly a hundred years. It was her ideal job and, as she wrote later, "what I feel very privileged about in my career is that I was in on the beginning of archaeozoology, and it has grown into quite a massive science".

She was based in the osteology room, which her colleague Caroline Grigson described as "a warren of mounted animal skeletons and assorted cupboards of bones" where she received and helped visiting researchers from all over the world with her "vast knowledge of mammalian osteology, zoological nomenclature and animal behaviour, while carrying on with her own analysis of material from archaeological sites

Juliet at work at the
National History Museum,
Peter Macdiarmid/The
Independent

in Britain, Switzerland, the Middle East and India, which resulted in the production of over 100 scientific papers."

For over 20 years, until her retirement in 1993, animal bones from archaeological excavations all over Britain flowed into her domain, where she meticulously processed, identified, analysed and wrote about them. As her friend the academic and author, Arthur MacGregor, wrote, "osteological research is in itself an exacting science, depending not only on a good eye and a retentive memory but also on considerable analytical capacities: to these objective skills Juliet was able to add a deep knowledge of living animal populations (and their human counterparts), accumulated during wide travels and allowing her to clothe the bare bones with flesh, hides and wool and to reanimate them both as independent living organisms and as essential adjuncts of human societies. These twin interests were acknowledged by her election to fellowships of both the Society of Antiquaries and the Zoological Society, while her contributions to scholarship were recognized with the award of a D.Sc. in 1991 by the University of London."

Her knowledge of bones was really remarkable and whenever the family went out for a walk – particularly in the fields and dunes around the cottage they bought in Cornwall – she'd bend over and pick up a little bleached white bone – and say this is the metatarsus or the ulna of a rabbit or a mouse.

Throughout her career Juliet was interested in domestic animals and she and Peter were founder members in 1973 of the Rare Breeds Survival Trust (RBST), which they helped set up with Joe Henson who ran Bemborough farm in the Cotswolds. In 1971 Joe and his wife Gilly opened up the Cotswolds Farm Park where they began breeding rare farm breeds, and the park proved to be a huge success with the public.

Joe's conservation work had began in 1969 when he agreed to provide a permanent home at his farm for Lord Zuckerman's "living gene bank", a collection of endangered farm animals temporarily housed at Whipsnade Zoo. Peter was a member of the initial working party set up by the zoo and the Royal Agricultural Society of England, and with his knowledge of the Soays and Juliet's interest in sheep, pigs and cows they were ideally placed to add scientific rigour to this new enterprise. They both enjoyed spending time at the farm park with Joe and Gilly and visiting their Gloucester cow, Molly, which they owned but Joe looked after. The RBST is still flourishing today as a conservation charity and since it was founded no UK-native farm breed has become extinct.

Juliet's interest in the recent history of farm animals resulted in a paper in The Agricultural History Review (1976) in which she described some models of "improved" livestock made in and after 1795 by the celebrated animal artist George Garrard, which she had found hidden away, and rather battered, in a cupboard in the Natural History Museum.

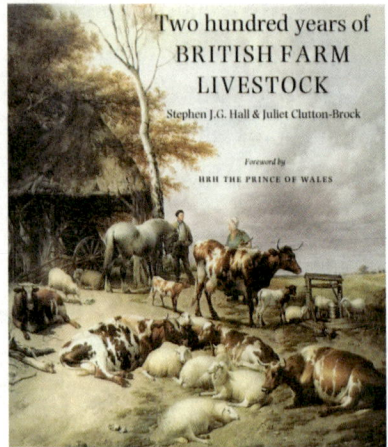

In collaboration with Stephen Hall, she wrote *Two Hundred Years of British Farm Livestock* (1989).

It was at this time that development of radio-carbon dating and the discovery of DNA gave a significant boost to archaeozoology, and Juliet worked closely with the British Museum's radio-carbon dating laboratory and Richard Burleigh to establish the age of the animal remains she was identifying. Archaeozoology was developing as a science, and in 1976 the International Council for Archaeozoology (ICAZ) was consolidated at a conference in Nice, and Juliet was chosen to be a member of the executive committee. The council organises international conferences every four years in various parts of the world – Juliet and her colleague, Caroline Grigson, organised the fourth conference at the Institute of Archaeology, in 1982. Many of the resulting conference papers, *Animals and Archaeology*, published in four volumes in 1983 and 1984, are still widely read. In 1988 Juliet edited *The Walking Larder: Patterns of Domestication, Pastoralism and Predation*, consisting of papers given at the World Archaeological Conference in Southampton in 1986. She attended many conferences all over the world, and sometimes took part in excavations, most notably at Abu Salabikh in Iraq in October 1977.

Throughout her career Juliet's main passion and interest was the domestication of the dog and she wrote at least 20 scientific papers on dogs and an 82-page paper, *A Review of the Family Canidae*, was published in 1976 by the Natural History Museum. She was a prolific writer and published over a hundred papers, and wrote (or edited) about 18 books, including *A Natural History of Domesticated Mammals* (1987), *Horse Power: a History of the Horse and Donkey in Human Societies* (1992), and the *Eyewitness Guides: Dog, Cat, Horse and Mammals*.

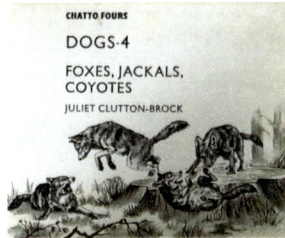

One of the first set of books Juliet published, 1970

# Lectures, giraffes and professorship: Peter's career progresses

# II

I n November 1967 Peter wrote to a colleague, Dr Matthews, ex-
plaining his situation: "You will know of the sequence of events
in Nigeria and you may have heard that I had to evacuate myself
and family in rather a hurry. We had to leave most things behind and of
course had to abandon the field work I had started. I must admit I was
surprised at how many angwantibos we saw and it is rather amusing that
an animal we thought to be rather rare and in need of 'conservation'
should turn out to be so common locally at least. I now face rather a serious situation as far as my work and a job are concerned, following the
collapse of the University College biological sciences link with the University of Nigeria, and I shall have to seek another post. In applying to
new posts may I give your name as a referee?"

After applying for various jobs Peter took up a post as senior lecturer and director of the master's degree course in conservation at the
Department of Zoology, University College London. Here he began
organising in earnest the study of large mammals in Africa. In 1970 he
started supervising the work of a Ugandan postgraduate student on the
reproductive behaviour of the topi, a large antelope, and was involved

Photographs Peter took of the Topi he studied in Uganda

in a scheme to domesticate antelope on the Galana Ranch in Kenya. He loved camping in the bush and enjoyed recounting his adventures – whether hiding from lions or being charged by elephants.

He wrote many letters to the family describing his adventures as in this one from the Nuffield Unit of Tropical Animal Ecology, Queen Elizabeth National Park, Lake Katwe, Uganda, where he was studying the topi.

*10 February 1970*

*My dearest little Sarah it is your time for a letter at last. I tried to write to you last night but had to give up because the mozzies were so bad; they are not so bad tonight because it is cooler. Also I didn't feel too good after a tin of Chinese salted black beans and curried rice that I had eaten, I think they were stale. Do you realise that I left London, and all you tiny nestlings on January 10 so already a month has gone by, just as I told you the time would fly so it has. Almost a third of my time gone already and hardly anything done. Before I know where I am it will be time to return. I am just drinking some of your favourite drink. Beer. I hope that you are allowed to have some now and again.*

*The days are rather strange here now because a lot of grass fires have been started and they fill the air with haze. Bits of burnt grass, black as charcoal, drift down on to us as I sit in the field. So far the open parts where my topi are have not been burnt. Now I will just look back at the three lovely letters you have sent me to see if there is anything I must answer. I love reading your letters, and read them over and over again as I have nothing else to read. I am doing my best to get interesting photos to show you – like a picture of lions eating a buffalo and of the skeleton afterwards.*

*It has gone 9 o'clock, 7 o'clock with you, and I shall now go to bed. I must remember to clean my teeth and get my things out ready for breakfast so that as soon as I have shooed away the elephant who eats the hedge in the morning I can get my breakfast without too much trouble in the pitch dark. So lots of love from the bush, Daddy P.S very interesting about the fox*

The fox he was referring to was a dead one that Juliet had found on her drive home across Hampstead Heath. Rebecca wrote to Peter about it:

*Dear Daddy,*
*I hope you are not going to be eaten by the mosquitos and thank you very much for your lovely letter. On Wednesday mummy came back from work quite late because on the way she found a dead fox it was not squashed so she picked it up and put it in the car boot. Now mummy found the fox where you found that squashed one and then when she got home she showed it to us. And so the next day she took it to the museum and they cut it up and used it as a skeleton otherwise they would burn it.*
*Love Rebecca*

On 16 March 1970 Peter wrote again from Uganda:

*My dearest little Sarah, I am always thinking of you and trying to get good pictures. I saw two vultures on a tree. Sarah would like to see those, I thought, and so I took a snap. A lovely little gecko is right by me eating the insects that fall off the lamp. He has just eaten a small cockroach and two beetles.*
*Lots of love Daddy.*

One of Peter's PhD students was Robin Pellew, who had done an MSc in Conservation. He describes Peter as a very charismatic character "compared with the other rather grey lecturers, here was someone in full technicolour – dynamic, funny, pretty chaotic, but with real passion for his subject". Robin remembers that the audience for his lectures was always huge: "Literally dozens of students, hanging on his every word, especially the young ladies in the front two rows – and he adored the adulation and would play up to it! I then got involved with him, as he was looking for a student to work on the domestication of musk-oxen in Alaska, which I started in about 1972 but which ended abruptly when all the calves at the domestication unit started dying of some mysterious infection and the farm was put in quarantine."

Robin began working on the demographics of giraffe in the Serengeti from 1974-79 with Peter as his supervisor. He describes how towards the end of his time in the Serengeti, Peter came out for a final supervision trip and they'd been out in the Land Rover all day and were heading back: "It was getting dark and the rain had been pelting down pretty hard all afternoon and when we came to the crossing of the Seronera River, it was dangerously flooded. To cross or not? With all the rain, the water level was clearly rising so we could be cut off from cold beers, hot food and comfortable beds for a

couple of days or more. Peter said we should wait but Pam [Robin's girlfriend] and I were in favour of trying it. A big mistake. Half way across the drift, the power of the wa-ter pushed us off the

Peter (standing, middle) looking at a giraffe he was tagging

concrete ramp and we crashed down into the bed of the river and were swept away. We all managed to get out OK and make it to the bank, although it was pretty frightening, but then we were faced with the reality of a five mile hike back to the Institute in the dark in the middle of the greatest concentration of wildlife in Africa – and the torch had been lost with the vehicle. Nothing for it but to set off in the rain, holding hands and trying to control a rising sense of panic. This changed to near hysteria when we were followed by a group of hyaenas – we could hear them giggling and their soft padding along the road behind us. Peter suggested singing might help – as if! – so on we strode with Peter leading us with a tremulous rendition of Onward Christian Soldiers. How this might have eventually worked out I don't know for we were saved by the lights of an approaching National Parks vehicle coming to check the water-level at the crossing."

Robin describes Peter as a very good head of department who pretty much left his postgrads to get on with things by themselves. "He was never pushy or pressurising, but would always give you advice or guidance when you needed it, but it was up to you to ask rather than wait for him to initiate any "supervision". As a supervisor, he was great at seeing the core issue that needed to be expanded for your thesis and what could be dropped maybe for a separate paper, but never ask him for advice about anything to do with statistics! He was great when assessing how a piece of work fitted into the bigger ecological picture, never getting too bogged down in the minutiae of the research. And his interests were genuinely broad ranging – ecology, reproductive-physiology, archaeozoology, domestication, you name it – so exceptionally stimulating to chew the fat with. I feel I owe Peter a big debt of gratitude as he took me on when I was a lot older than his other students, having spent several years with a job outside university after graduating, and in many ways he was my mentor during that Serengeti time."

In 1972 Peter was offered the post of professor of zoology at Royal Holloway College, University of London. He started the job on 1 October 1972 – at a salary of £6,036 a year. He made his inaugural lecture on 14

Photograph of a giraffe taken by Peter in the Serengeti

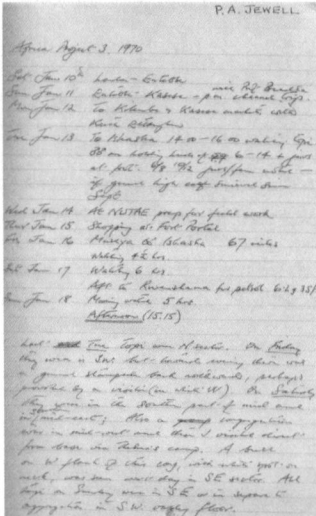
Peter's research on the Topi, 1970

February 1972 and it was titled *Male and Female*. In his introduction to his lecture he talked about "an announcement of signal importance in zoology", which had occurred in the previous year when the Nobel Prize for Medicine was awarded to three men who were students of animal behaviour – Konrad Lorenz, Karl von Frish and Niko Tinbergen – and who founded the new science of ethology, the comparative study of animal behaviour, with a focus on behaviour under natural conditions. Their first discoveries were made on insects, fish and birds, but the basic principles proved to be applicable also to mammals, including man. In his lecture, Peter spoke about how he hoped this event would mark the end of an era of prejudice against ethological studies and open the door to new researches that would lead, he believed, "to some of the brightest discoveries to be made in biology".

He went on to describe how, post-Darwin, field studies "went into the doldrums – it was felt to be work for amateurs and was even scorned. Through the decades of the 1920s, 30s and 40s therefore, little was done except by a few pioneers." In Africa, he said, "the living panorama of evolution that persisted in the great herds of game animals was virtually unstudied. The elephant was ignored until 5-10 years ago, rhinoceros, buffalo, giraffe – there is no monograph on their behaviour."

Peter went on to say: "It's naive to suppose that this turning away was simply a question of fashion in science, other factors were at work. Particularly religious prejudice. A too-close study would blur the distinction between man and the rest of the animal kingdom. Nor were scientists immune from the political attitudes of the countries they lived in. Just as imperial nations exploited the native peoples of the colonies so biologists exploited the animals."

He goes on to describe how it wasn't until the post-war period that there was a new spirit of liberation that infected zoology, and behaviourists and psychologists all realised the wealth of information to be discovered

A Soay sheep, photographed by Peter

– particularly in primates. And Peter was part of this movement and was determined to start his own field studies. "I decided to focus on our own doorstep and look at one of the largest mammals that Britain had to offer – the Soay sheep in the Hebrides. I knew feral populations on St Kilda that no one had studied and I had an ulterior motive – they were a simple model. That was in 1959. Later I went to Africa and studied the most charming of antelopes – the Topi. I do not presume to suggest that the work I have done has any particular bearing on the behaviour of man. But I do believe that ethological studies in general and comparisons between the behaviour of animals and man will have a great bearing on our understanding of our psychology and, therefore, in the long run on our happiness."

While professor at Royal Holloway he worked on a project looking at tourism in Uganda and wrote a report about his findings in 1972, in which he said: "If the fundamental cultural, scientific and economic reasons for conserving wildlife and protecting areas of scenic beauty are accepted, then their exploitation for tourism is a rational use. Safeguards are needed to ensure that this exploitation is not short-term but that an enduring asset is maintained." He was critically aware of the importance of preserving ecosystems and his report has as much relevance today: "Man has so altered every biome of the globe that only remnants are left of the complex and specialised communities of wild animals and plants that evolved to take advantage of every kind of environment. These communities still conceal a vast store of species, and of productive systems, that man has now studied and that he by-passed when he selected a few special ways of food production and of using a limited number of natural products." Peter went on to talk about the growing concern in the world for conservation that inspired Uganda, and 34 other African states, to sign the African Convention on the Conservation of Nature and Natural Resources.

Peter worked at Royal Holloway for five years from 1972-77 while living at Hollycroft Avenue, in Hampstead, where he and Juliet had bought a house. But he hated the commute – it was a long drive to the Royal Holloway campus in Egham, Surrey, and he'd come home exhausted and eventually became depressed. He often used to sit in his armchair mute and unable to speak, and although he was enjoying his work he began looking around for other jobs.

After a number of unsuccessful applications, including to the Food and Agriculture Organization of the United Nations and the Nature Conservancy Council, on 1 October 1977, to his great delight, he was appointed Mary Marshall and Arthur Walton Professor of Physiology of Reproduction at the University of Cambridge. He also became a

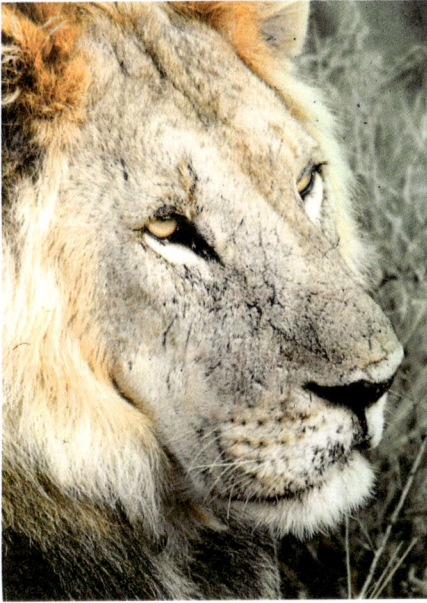
Lion photograph taken by Peter

fellow of St John's College, where he had been a student, and threw himself whole-heartedly into Cambridge life. Robert Hinde, who was Master of St John's college wrote: "Peter sat for a while on the College Council, and served on a number of college committees. His enthusiasm and his ability to listen, assimilate and reply made any discussion with him a pleasure: his unfailing good-humour and his kindness to both peers and juniors formed a lasting impression on all who knew him."

Now that Peter was based in Cambridge, he and Juliet decided to buy a small house so he could live there during the week and after much searching they bought 36 Hertford street, a pretty terraced house that Peter filled with art, pottery and African artefacts that he collected and loved. He really adored being a professor at Cambridge – he felt real recognition at last of his work and he enjoyed all the pomp and circumstance of college life. His work on the Soay sheep continued and also his supervision of PhD students and their studies of giraffe and grazing ruminants in Tanzania; leopards in Kenya; pastoralists and their cattle in Ethiopia and sheep in England.

Stephen Hall, one of Peter's research students, has many happy memories of his days at Cambridge and he dedicated his book, *Live-*

*stock Biodiversity: Genetic Resources for the Farming of the Future*, to Peter, describing him as "a most valued friend, and inspiring mentor and colleague".

Stephen worked with Peter recording the mating patterns of sheep. On one project he remembered the rams were called Teddy, Ali, Cecil and Larry. "Needless to say, we organised the timings of matings so rams had time to recover and also we ensured that rams were used evenly across all matings. Peter's belief was that each of the rams (respectively Southdown, Shropshire, Suffolk and Leicester Longwool) would stamp his breed characteristics (colour and fleece type) on the lambs."

The following spring they inspected the lambs and assigned parentage primarily by blood typing (resemblance to putative sires proved to be unreliable as an indicator of paternity) and sure enough, said Stephen, "as hypothesised from the St. Kilda observations the 64 lambs born were the progeny of mating times as follows: 2 at 3 hours, 27 at 9 hours, 23 at 15 hours and 12 at 21 hours. It was a really nice example of field observation leading to hypothesis duly tested experimentally and was published in the Journal of Reproduction and Fertility in 1986."

From 1971-1979 Peter was vice chairman of the Mammal Society. The society was set up, he later wrote, to enable all kinds of people interested in British mammals to "get together, exchange information, give papers on what they had been doing, learn more about methods of studying mammals, and actually see and learn to handle the less conspicuous ones". In the early days, the enthusiasts who attended the annual weekend get-together were particularly pleased to see Longworth traps in action and handle species of rodents and shrews that many had never actually seen, and similarly handle bats for the first time, caught in mist nets. It is hard to remember, he wrote, "how little was known about our mammalian fauna at that time and that all these activities provided new and exciting information. I saw the role of the Society as entirely positive and as laying the ground for serving the interests of mammals in Britain. This is because we were arming young people with vital facts about the natural history and needs of mammals."

From 1986-91 he was chairman of the Mammal Society and in 1991 he became its president. He also served on numerous academic committees, acting as a consultant in Britain and abroad, and assisting in surveys by the Overseas Development Administration and the EEC on proposals for the integrated development of the Omo-Turkana region, Ethiopia and Kenya. In 1989 he wrote another book, *The Biology of Large African Mammals in their Environment.*

Peter with a buffalo in the Masai Mara, Kenya

# School days and holidays: family life in Highgate, Hampstead and Gwithian

I am Peter and Juliet's eldest daughter and have so many happy memories of growing up with my sisters in Highgate and Hampstead. The family first lived at 36 Southwood Lane, Highgate, where Vanessa Topsy was born in 1961 and Rebecca Tamsin in 1963. As the family expanded, the house quickly became too small and a few years later we moved one street away to 45 Jackson's Lane.

Peter and Juliet were loving and devoted parents, but in different ways. Juliet was strict and regimented – everything was done to routine and rules, and everyone had to pull their weight and help with chores. Once she started working full-time and us three girls were at school we had a three-week rota for making breakfast – one week was spent laying the table the night before, another week getting up to make breakfast, and then a week off. Breakfast was always cereal one day followed by boiled eggs the next day.

Juliet was strict but also very kind, and if we were sad or upset she was always loving and sympathetic. Rebecca remembers: "Whenever I was unhappy she would say 'come and sit on my lap and be my baby' and she would cuddle me and make me feel better."

Peter didn't care about living by the rule book – he was a free spirit but had a terrible temper and it wasn't a good idea to anger him. But he was always compassionate and caring; I remember when I was ill that he'd sit next to the bed and hold my hand, reading me stories.

I also vividly recall not wanting to go to school and sitting on Peter's knee in our house in Jackson's Lane, and him cuddling me as I was crying and him telling me not to be upset, and saying listen to my new record – it was Joni Mitchell and was so sad and beautiful it made me cry even more.

Juliet relaxing in the back garden, Jackson's Lane

Peter and Juliet both enjoyed listening to music and had a big collection of records – Juliet loved the great folk singers of the 60s, Joan Baez, Bob Dylan and Donovan. But her real love was Mozart, Beethoven and Bach, particularly choral

The dining room in Jackson's Lane

works and opera. Peter listened to more rock and jazz – Janis Joplin, the Beetles and Ella Fitzgerald. They enjoyed playing their records while entertaining and Topsy remembers: "We girls used to sit on the stairs and spy on their dinner parties through the gaps in the staircase, and in the morning we'd get up early and pretend to be smoking on the cigarette ends and drink the dregs from their wine glasses."

In 1962 Peter and Juliet made an impulsive decision – to buy a house in Cornwall, as Juliet had long craved for an escape from London. Their good friends Charles and Jessica Thomas, who they met through their shared love of archaeology, lived in Gwithian, near Hayle on the north coast in the St Ives Bay, and one day Jessica rang to say that a house on the hill overlooking the village was for sale. The owner, who was a pig farmer, had been bitten by one of his pigs and got septicaemia and died.

The cottage, Gwithian in 1963

Juliet made one of her infamous snap decisions and decided they must buy it. So began the family's long and lasting love affair with the north Cornish coast.

The couple had a Bedford van and, for every holiday, they bundled us children into it for the 13-hour drive to the cottage. There was no electricity and the house was lit by calor gas mantle lights on the ground floor. The gas was delivered in cylinders by Bennetts in Camborne and stood in a concrete hut outside the kitchen. Upstairs we used candles and paraffin lamps – Peter was in charge of the lamps and the paraffin, and used to cut

Peter reading a story in Jackson's Lane

the wicks and fill them up every evening.

There was a rayburn stove in the dining room and a wood burning fireplace in the sitting room but no other heating. The house when my parents first bought it had earth floors but they laid jaunty black and white lino tiles and papered the front room in William Morris's pretty daisy design wallpaper. There was no running water, and the water from the bore hole outside often came out of the taps a murky brown.

The semi-detached house overlooks an acre field that gently undulates down towards the village and the sea. You can see the sunset over the sea and rolling waves from the house. The beach – "three miles of golden sands" – is one of the most beautiful on the north coast. The local lighthouse off Godrevy cove is the one that Virginia Woolf wrote about in her novel To the Lighthouse. It was an idyllic spot that both Peter and Juliet loved and cherished their whole lives.

Meanwhile, back in London, we were well settled into our new house in Jackson's Lane. It was one of a row of flat-fronted modern 1960s houses that had just been built, with attractive white-wooden cladding and wide, rectangular windows. The house was all open plan with beautiful polished wooden floors and big open wooden stairs.

Peter and Juliet were one of many young couples who all moved in around the same time with their babies, and we became firm friends with John and Bobby Weeks, Brian and Pat Adams, and Bob and Hannah Gavron, and all their respective children. It was a real community of neighbours and everyone had dinner parties in each other's houses and used to run a walkie talkie intercom with wires out of the windows from one house to another to hear if the children were crying.

All of the gardens were joined by a path that ran along the back and we children used to climb trees and have tea parties under the rhododendron bushes. The highlight of the year was Guy Fawke's night – everyone bought fireworks and lit a bonfire and ate baked potatoes while Peter and the other dads set off huge rockets. We girls were happy at Highgate primary school and life was idyllic.

Then our family moved to Nigeria and the security and cosiness of the Jackson's Lane bubble was burst. When we came back to London in 1967 secondary school was looming and Juliet decided that we needed to move again to be nearer a secondary school. Her aunt Doreen generously

Topsy and Lucie, Sarah and Rags, Rebecca and Moppet

gave her some money to help her buy a bigger home. They started looking in Hampstead, and 21 Hollycroft Avenue – a large Edwardian, redbrick, semi-detatched house – came up at auction. Peter, ever the impulsive gambler who loved a challenge, went along, bid for it and bought it for £32,000, and then regretted it for the rest of his life. It was a beautiful house but it was in the middle of the bourgeois desert, as Peter called Hampstead and its suburban environs. He complained that he had no study and no privacy in the house and there was no community outside.

Despite his protestations, we all settled into family life in a much bigger house – each of us girls had her own bedroom and we all had space to spread out. Juliet's living room was on the ground floor and beautifully decorated with William Morris curtains and dusty green walls and her mahogany writing desk; Peter had his stuffed birds and a huge print of Darwin on the wall over the French wood-burning stove. Upstairs we girls had the "brown room" – (two rooms that had been turned by the previous owners into one huge room that ran from the front to the back of the house). We had a TV, sofa and a full-size ping pong table, and many happy hours were spent entertaining our friends there.

My friend from school, Caroline Labrum, has vivid memories of hanging out in Hollycroft Avenue. The first time she came to the house was for my birthday party in 1973, and she remembers: "There was a big privet hedge archway over the front gate and a tortoise – Frederika – was walking across the lawn in the front garden and eating a cucumber slice".

She rang the doorbell and heard the dog – Rags, my Yorkshire terrier, and Lucie, Topsy's white and tan cross breed terrier, barking: "Peter opened the door and about six or seven of Lucie's puppies came scampering around me which was the most delightful thing I could ever have imagined." The house was always full of animals – as well as the dogs there was Moppet the tabby cat, goldfish and catfish in a large tank, stick insects, two pet rats, two tortoises and Honey the hamster.

Peter loved entertaining and he always hosted our birthday parties and thought up the most brilliant games. Caroline remembers, in particular, a penny auction: "Everyone was given a purse and we had to hunt for pennies that were hidden around the house and when they were all found Peter sat us in his study and did an auction of various trinkets and toys. I'd never experienced anything like that and it was absolutely fabulous."

We also played another game devised by Peter where we children had to walk around the room blindfolded and try to hit a balloon in the air with one of his ties. Caroline remembers Peter as always being "crazy, jokey and fun – he was always messing around and loved teasing us – but he was always interested in everyone as well and would ask me questions about myself".

She recalls Juliet as being a more distant, quite intimidating figure who spent time in her sitting room playing Mozart or choral works, and in the evenings always had a glass of whisky on the go: "I was in awe of Juliet and had to be respectful and on my best behaviour with her." She remembered staying the night and having to creep upstairs because Juliet was a very light sleeper, "and we were always told not to flush the lavatory so as not to wake Juliet up". In the morning Juliet was always the first up and she'd let the dogs out and then the dogs would come and jump into bed with us, which wasn't allowed but was tolerated.

Meals were eaten in the kitchen which had a big yellow Aga and we children used to sit on the round metal covers over the hot plates. Eventually they both had dents in them – much to Juliet's annoyance – but the Aga kept the kitchen warm and the dog baskets were beneath it to keep the dogs toasty during the winter. There was a big round oak table with 1960s Magistretti chairs bought from Heals around it.

We had a roast every Sunday after a walk on the heath and a pint in the pub – Jack Straw's Castle or Spaniard's Inn. Juliet was a good cook and made lovely meals, Caroline remembers that she made unusual and different food, "one time she was making pesto out of pine nuts and basil – and this was way before it became a staple of supermarket shopping".

I remember that growing up we had a lot of freedom to do as we wanted, and had quite a wild time as my parents were busy with their own lives. We had a long succession of au pairs who were supposed to be in charge of us but really weren't. Peter's career was taking off and when he became a professor in Cambridge he started living part-time in London. Juliet was working full-time, unlike many mothers during that era, and travelling the world with her archaeozoology friends. Caroline remembers me declaring proudly: "My mum is doing a man's job – no other women have that responsibility."

Juliet never declared herself a feminist but she fought hard to have parity with her male colleagues, and when the museum tried to make her redundant she successfully fought for her position and won after a long and protracted dispute. Juliet held quite liberal views about our boyfriends and relationships – she always said she didn't mind boys coming over and staying the night – just don't get pregnant.

After moving to Hampstead we missed the community spirit of Highgate at first, but we soon became engrossed in our new school life at South Hampstead High School – a strict, academic, all-girls school in south Hampstead that got excellent results but had a stifling post-Victorian atmosphere and treated its pupils as fodder to be fed through the academic exams machine. The mistresses were an eccentric bunch – they were mainly a lot of elderly, very strict, other-worldly women – as illustrated by the infamous occasion when a builder who had come to fix the windows in Rebecca's classroom started flashing the girls who were sitting in orderly

The family at the house in Jackson's Lane, 1970

rows around him. Hysteria broke out but the teacher didn't notice anything amiss going on and told the girls to be quiet.

The equally infamous Mademoiselle Muller, who was know as Mademoiselle, inspired fear in all pupils and ruled with a rod of iron – if you got your French conjugation verbs wrong you got a slap across the hand with the ruler. The pupils were cooped up inside with very little space outside – there was a tiny little concrete playground, which was surrounded by high fences and the only real exercise was tennis in Belsize Park or walking to Regent's Park to play hockey.

The regimented weekdays were relieved by the fun of the weekends when we as a family went on exciting day trips. Peter loved to drive into the countryside for a picnic in summer (just as his father had done) and they spent many happy times at the Cotswold Farm Park in Gloucestershire or visiting Alan and Barbara at Chastleton.

We also spent a lot of time with Peter's sister Pamela, her husband Tom and their four children, Karen, Anna, Guy and Edward. Our two families are still close today. Pam and Tom lived in a big house next to

Kew Gardens and always had a houseful of visitors, live-in guests and pets – including their Soay sheep Harold who ran around the kitchen leaving his droppings behind him.

As we girls grew older, the day trips became less frequent and life was complicated by the fact that Peter and Juliet essentially had an open marriage. Peter had always had affairs with other women and Juliet had a long-term relationship that lasted many years. They were quite open with each other about these extra-marital relationships and tolerated them, but there was a lot of tension at home, particularly when Peter came back at weekends after living in Cambridge during the week and they had both been seeing their other partners.

We children were quite often left on our own as Juliet had lots of friends abroad through her work and frequently travelled to Israel, the Netherlands, Germany and Denmark. Peter was often away in Africa working and we were never quite sure who was going to be where when. Rebecca remembers Juliet writing to the headmistress to say that she and Peter would be away and the girls would be on their own. As Rebecca recalls: "I felt proud that we were going to have to look after ourselves and my friends were very impressed and rather amazed."

Robin Pellew, one of Peter's PhD students, remembers one occasion when he and his wife Pam were invited to dinner at Hollycroft Avenue: "Obviously some important couple had dropped out and we were last minute stand-ins. The company that assembled for the pre-dinner drinks was pretty powerful, with masters of colleges, professors of this and that, fellows of the Royal Society – and us! The curious feature of the evening was the non-appearance of Juliet who we naively believed was slaving over a hot stove in the kitchen – we didn't know her very well then!"

Peter entertained the company with several stories and copious quantities of booze while surreptitiously glancing at his watch as the time passed. They all got more and more drunk as the evening wore on "with no wife and no food". Then at about 10pm, Robin remembers: "The door flew open and in walked Juliet who seemed totally non-plussed to find her living-room full of strangers. Peter then made the fatal mistake of asking her if there was any food, which prompted a violent explosion: 'You asked all these wretched people so you can damn-well feed them', with which she turned and walked out the front door. It was absolutely brilliant! Peter was completely thrown, desperately phoning Indian take-aways, while Pam and I just collapsed in laughter – but then the door-bell never stopped ringing with vast quantities of food delivered by a dozen takeaways and we had a very jolly meal."

Holidays were always spent at the cottage in Cornwall and one of the family's favourite places to go for long windswept walks was along the dramatic cliffs at Zennor – followed by a pint of real ale in the village at the Tinner's Arms. On the drive along the clifftop, one of the famous landmarks is Eagle's Nest – the former home of the artist Patrick Heron, who Peter really admired. It's a beautiful granite house whose history is intertwined with our family.

In 1921 Will Arnold-Forster, the painter and politician, bought Eagle's Nest and began planting a spectacular garden around the huge granite boulders that sit like giant eggs overlooking the patchwork quilt of ancient tiny fields and dry-stone walls that stretch out to the sea. Will was married to Katherine "Ka" Cox (born 1887) – who famously had an affair with Rupert Brooke and was a friend of Virginia Woolf. Their only son Mark inherited Eagle's Nest and subsequently sold it in 1955 to one of his best friends – Patrick Heron. Mark Arnold-Forster is the father of Jake Arnold-Forster who is Rebecca's husband.

Rebecca has many happy memories of walking along the cliff tops at Zennor and also how one winter when it was very windy "we drove up to the headland and I got out of the car and was blown over flat into a puddle!". She also remembers swimming and "surfing in the sea with our plywood surf boards and then eating delicious crunchy apples afterwards as we shivered from the cold".

Topsy recalls dramatic cliff top walks and one in particular: "Dad took us on a walk that started up the lane behind the house and made a circuit around to the cliffs at Hells Mouth. He worked out the route on a map and knew we would have to cross some fields with no footpath. We had our dogs Rags and Lucie with us, and when we came to the field we saw a dairy herd. I don't know if Dad noticed the bull when we entered the field, but with a stout walking stick in hand he marched us all on.

"When the black and white bull came towards us and started pawing the ground I remember the feeling of rising panic. Mum and Dad tried shooing him away by waving their sticks. This did little to deter the angry bull and it was clear that he was going to charge. Dad told us children to scramble on to the hedge pulling the dogs with us. We all managed to clamber over the hedge into another field and safety. I still have nightmares of coming across wild beasts and clambering on hedges to escape!"

These were such happy times for us all. Whatever we did with Peter and Juliet it was exciting, and together as a family we had so many adventures.

# Retirement, Cambridge and the Fens: the final years

# 13

In 1992 Peter retired from his professorship at Cambridge and when Juliet retired from the Natural History Museum in 1993 they decided to sell the Hollycroft Avenue house and the one at Hertford Street, Cambridge, and buy an bigger home near Cambridge.

They found a beautiful converted barn in Fen Ditton on the east side of Cambridge that was perfect for them. It had been converted in the 1970s and had large picture windows, a central log-burning fireplace and huge high-ceilinged airy rooms. The large garden had a walnut tree in the centre of it and Juliet had a dovecote made and started breeding white doves that fluttered around and sat cooing on the roof tiles. They also had a small flock of bantam hens and ate the eggs for breakfast. The garden overlooked the river Cam and there was a herd of cows grazing in the surrounding fields that gave an idyllic, peaceful feel to the whole place. They loved having friends and family, including their nine grandchildren, to stay, and walking in the wide open fenland of Cambridgeshire.

Peter was enjoying his retirement, still a fellow of St John's College, travelling to meetings abroad and entertaining friends. He carried on actively interested in the conservation of large mammals and in October

Juliet and Peter

1995 organised and chaired a meeting in Rome, funded by the International Fund for Animal Welfare, on elephants in Africa – looking at the problems of poaching, population control, culling, and the relationship between elephants and farmers and villagers. Juliet attended as well and the meeting notes recorded: "It was agreed that due to their close and integrated social structure, long-term memory, size and great longevity and their capacity for long-distance communication, it is impossible to kill elephants humanely." A long list of recommendations resulted – support for Amboseli park in Kenya as an elephant sanctuary, support for the enlargement of Addo Elephant National Park in South Africa and support for research into improving ways of containing elephant populations, including contraception in females, the creation of an international African elephant research and management group, and strengthening the ban on international trade in ivory.

This was to be Peter's last conservation meeting about animal welfare in Africa, as in early 1996 he became ill with a chest infection and developed pneumonia. But in April he wrote to his old friend Sydney Holt saying he was a bit better: "I am feeling somewhere near my old self. Not my old self as I used to be in my youth – oh no, don't go away with that idea. My old self now is – old. The good thing is having your friends and close pals and books about and abandoning all silly bourgeois conventions and eating off the table without a plate and taking your socks off when you feel too hot and so on. I am engrossed in reading a biography of William Morris – a very fat book and me a very slow reader. It's a magical read and evokes that feeling for socialism that too often gets buried and lost in disappointment."

He goes on to invite Sydney to stay in the two places he loves; "Come and spend time here in this old barn that I think you will like very much, relaxing at the edge of the English fens. Eating, drinking real ale, resting, gentle walks, visits to Wicken Fen and Woodwalton Fen. Hear the cuckoo and talk to the dogs and doves. Or come to Cornwall and stay with us in our cottage. Constant sea views, bracing cliff walks, stimulating air, eating, drinking real ale."

Peter recovered from the pneumonia but the following year was diagnosed with cancer of the pancreas and died on 23 May 1998, aged 72. One of his students, Dr Nick Tyler, wrote about him: "Peter was in the vanguard of the movement that turned ecology and animal behaviour into respectable sciences worthy of study at a time when these subjects were not taken seriously. His work with the Soay sheep of St Kilda is still going on and a lot of very bright people moved in and have applied field methods and analytical techniques that were never dreamed of in the 1960s.

"I doubt anyone reads *Island Survivors* any more but the phrase 'standing on the shoulders of giants' could never be better applied than in this regard."

The barn, Fen Ditton

Juliet carried on working after Peter died. Although she had retired from the Natural History Museum, she became one of the editors of the Journal of Zoology and from 1999 to 2006 was its managing editor. This was a very satisfying and enjoyable job for her – she was a very good editor, paying great attention to detail and she could focus on her concern for animal welfare. In 2003 she wrote: "As an Editor of the Journal of Zoology I welcome debate on issues to do with welfare science. Just as toe-clipping [where the toe is cut off completely] has been mostly replaced by the recording of individual patterns for recognition, so there are always new designs and improvements to be made in any research procedure. Perhaps the way forward is for an assessment of the possible negative effects of intervention on individual animals to be included as an integral part of all research projects. This should be as routine a procedure as other forms of risk assessment are becoming in managing impacts on human health and welfare.

She also carried on writing, and published a further 25 scientific papers, as well as book reviews for The Times Literary Supplement. She also became an associate editor of the Archives of Natural History. Her last book, *Animals as Domesticates: A World View Through History*, was published in 2012.

One of the last lectures she gave was at the Seventh International Theriological Congress, held at Acapulco in Mexico in 1997 where she gave a talk entitled The Wild and the Tame in the Past and the Present. In it she described the role of the archaeozoologist as not only providing answers to questions about how people and animals interacted in the past, "but also persuading conservationists that if they are to achieve a proper balance in the preservation of ecosystems they must take into account human environments on equal terms with the 'natural world'."

For most of history in the European-speaking world, she said, uncultivated lands and forests were enemy territory full of ferocious wild animals and imaginary demons. "It is only in the last 200 years, since all the so-called 'wild' places have been explored and penetrated by people travelling out from industrial centres of the Eurocentric world that nature and the wilderness have been sanctified."

She went on to say: "We all know that biologists will have to tackle increasingly in the future the great problems of how to manage the wild places and their faunas. It doesn't matter whether these faunas include African elephants, Asian lions, or giant tortoises, they will become increasingly hedged in and the wild will merge with the tame." Wildlife must be preserved, she said, "but so too must the declining breeds of domesticated animals, which over thousands of years have become perfectly adapted to their environments and have helped to shape landscapes, be they the downlands of northern Europe or the grasslands of North America."

In 2014 Juliet became ill and was diagnosed with cancer of the sinus, she bravely battled her illness but she died at the barn with her family and Sylvie, her dog, beside her, on 21 September 2015, five days after her 82nd birthday. She is buried next to Peter in the graveyard at Fen Ditton.

WS - #0131 - 140322 - C41 - 197/132/10 - PB - 9781784567866 - Matt Lamination

WS - #0131 - 140322 - C41 - 197/132/10 - PB - 9781784567866 - Matt Lamination